I Am ~~Miss D~~

Amy Dunne

I Am ~~Miss D~~

~~Amy Dunne~~

A VERY
PRIVATE TRAGEDY,
A VERY PUBLIC
CASE

AMY DUNNE

WITH ORLA O'DONNELL

Gill Books

Gill Books

Hume Avenue

Park West

Dublin 12

www.gillbooks.ie

Gill Books is an imprint of M.H. Gill and Co.

9780717190980

Design and print origination by O'K Graphic Design, Dublin

Edited by Emma Dunne

Proofread by Sally Vince

Printed by CPI Group (UK) Ltd, Croydon, CR0 4YY

This book is typeset in 18/20 pt Sabon.

A CIP catalogue record for this book is available from the British Library.

5 4 3 2 1

MIX
Paper from
responsible sources
FSC www.fsc.org   FSC® C171272

*Dedicated to all those who have fought
for their rights and what is right;
to everyone who has spoken out;
and to everyone who has suffered in silence.*

Amy Dunne is the woman who was known as 'Miss D' during a High Court case in 2007 in which she fought for her right to travel for an abortion. **Orla O'Donnell** is the legal affairs correspondent for RTÉ.

CONTENTS

PREFACE   IX

PROLOGUE   I

1   CHILDHOOD   5

2   RUNNING WILD   28

3   PREGNANT   55

4   COURT   81

5   DECISION TIME   107

6   LIVERPOOL   131

7   AFTERMATH   156

8   NEW BEGINNINGS   179

9   ESCAPING THE PAST   199

10   SHAME   219

11   I AM AMY DUNNE   244

ACKNOWLEDGEMENTS   265

PREFACE

When I reported on the case of 'Miss D' in May 2007, I had been Legal Affairs Correspondent for RTÉ News for less than a year.

The story of a 17-year-old girl in the care of the state, whose baby could not survive after birth but who was being prevented from travelling to the UK for an abortion, made headlines around the world and was one of the biggest cases I had ever reported on.

Every day, we broadcast live for the 1 p.m., 6 p.m. and 9 p.m. news bulletins. We usually reported from just outside our office near the Four Courts. We were raised slightly above street level, looking back at the courts across the busy road and the red Luas line.

Frequently, my reporting would have to battle with the noise of traffic, of trams trundling over the tracks, of irate tram drivers beeping at the cars blocking the line. I also had to compete with the sirens of garda cars and ambulances, which always seemed to time their journeys to coincide with the moment the news anchor introduced me from studio.

Because of the nature of live television reporting and the logistics involved, I usually had to leave court every day before the proceedings finished for lunch to give myself enough time to get into position. In the evenings, I had to rush off when the case ended to write TV scripts and radio reports. There was little time to stand around and get to know people or to process the day's events

I was eager to do a good job and anxious to make sure everything I broadcast was accurate. I thought I had done that. But I heard from a colleague that Miss D herself was very upset at the reports broadcast on the news. Later, I read interviews where she said she had been 'destroyed' by the media coverage and in particular by having her personal details broadcast to the nation.

I was reporting what was said in court as I thought a good reporter should do. It never occurred to me that repeating what was said about Miss D and her family, no matter how accurately I had recorded the lawyers' words, would cause her great distress. As I grew older and more experienced, I wondered from time to time whether there was anything I could have done differently to have more consideration for the person at the heart of such a traumatic legal drama.

I realised that evidence given in court can sound much harsher when repeated out loud by a broadcaster. The effect is intensified when the reporter is on the side of the road, making herself heard over traffic and trams. These days, I always try to remember that at the heart of every legal challenge is a person, often a person who is suffering. I try not to add to that distress with my reporting.

In 2018, I saw an article on the BBC website about the upcoming referendum to repeal the eighth amendment to the constitution. It featured 28-year-old Amy Dunne speaking about her time as Miss D and the effect those events had on her. I had never spoken to her before, but I got in touch and told her that I wanted to apologise to her and her mother for any added upset I had caused them with my reports. She replied immediately and said it meant a lot to her.

Later on that year, I began working with film-maker Paddy Hayes and producer Aisling Ní Fhlaithearta on the *Finné* documentary series for TG4. The series focused on people who had been at the heart of newsworthy events and allowed them to tell their stories directly to camera. It occurred to me that Amy might have something to say about her time at the centre of a high-profile court case.

We met for a coffee to discuss the idea and despite the fact that I had reported on the case I was stunned into silence as she told her story. There was so much I hadn't known. And it seemed incredible to me that she had been put through this ordeal in 2007, in a supposedly modern society. It was also amazing that she had survived it so well. It would have been shocking for any young teenager, in such circumstances, to have been given the diagnosis she received for her baby. She suffered an even greater trauma by becoming the subject of a national debate, with the whole country weighing in on what she should or shouldn't do.

The documentary was positively received, and Amy later told a journalist from the *Guardian* that she felt 'reborn'. But her account of the tragic events of 2007 and their aftermath was only a fraction of what Amy had to say. So when I was asked to help her write her story for this book, I hoped I could finally make up for the upset I caused her all those years ago.

It has been a privilege to work with Amy on writing this book. It is a story of strength and resilience, pride and empathy, of overcoming shame and adversity to survive and build a full and vibrant life. It is also the story of how Amy Dunne, and her country, have changed beyond recognition in the years since she was Miss D.

Orla O'Donnell

PROLOGUE

'My baby! My baby!' My screams rang out as I was wheeled through the corridors of the Liverpool Women's Hospital.

It was the morning of 19 May 2007. I had given birth just hours earlier. Now I was being rushed out to catch a ten o'clock flight back to Dublin, drugged, bleeding, in agony.

I grabbed at the walls but there was nothing I could cling on to. I screamed for my baby again. I didn't want to leave. I was going home to Ireland and leaving my child behind.

At the nurses' station, they looked at me in horror and with sympathy. I grabbed the hands of the nurse I had come to know best. 'Don't leave her on her own,' I begged her. 'Please don't let her be on her own.' The nurse had tears in her eyes. She tried to smile and told me she'd look after my daughter.

I had left Jasmine, my little girl, alone in a hospital room.

My heart already ached for her, yet I had not seen her face. She had been born at almost 20 weeks and had never taken a breath outside my body. I had been induced after she was diagnosed with a rare condition that meant she was missing most of her skull and brain and could not survive outside the womb.

At the age of 17, and in the temporary care of the state after my relationship with my mother had broken down, I fought a legal battle to be allowed to come to Liverpool to end my pregnancy. This was not permitted in Ireland, unless there was a risk to the mother's life.

When I was told, just hours after the birth, that we had to pack up and catch our flight back home, I was out of my mind with exhaustion and morphine. I didn't get time to recover and to process my emotions. I was too scared to hold my tiny, fragile baby's body, too terrified to lift the blanket covering her head and to look at her little face. It was a fear that would torment me for years afterwards.

I have lived most of my adult life under a dark cloud of shame, carrying so much blame for everything that happened to me and to Jasmine. I was ashamed of becoming pregnant at 16, ashamed of being spoken about across the world as the anonymous Miss D at the centre of another controversial abortion case in the Irish courts. I was ashamed of my baby's fatal condition and thought it was all my fault. I was ashamed of what I felt was my immaturity and lack of responsibility – ashamed of failing to eat enough vegetables and not taking folic acid before getting pregnant.

I was ashamed, most of all, that I had gone to England to end what had been a much-wanted pregnancy. In 2007, I felt like I was the only woman in Ireland who had ever needed to travel for an abortion. I believed the whole country was talking about me, and it affected every relationship in my life. The shame only started to disappear more than a decade later, when Irish people voted in favour of changing the constitution. The debate around removing the words that specifically protected the unborn and prohibited abortion opened my eyes to the fact that I was not alone. I slowly began to forgive myself a little and to look at life in a different way. I realised I had spent years needlessly carrying all the blame and guilt for everything I had gone through. I began to reassess how I had been treated by the state, and by others, and to wonder if things could have been done very differently.

Whenever I look back on my situation, I always see two paths. There was the path I could have taken where there would have been no court case, no controversy. On this path I would have found out my baby wasn't well; I would have gone to England weeks earlier, had an abortion and returned home. If I had been allowed to take this route, I would not have built a connection with my daughter and losing her would not have been so traumatic. Nobody outside my family would ever have known my story. My private grief would have remained private.

But the path I had to take was very different. It involved judges, lawyers, and a very public debate in which my decision to travel was discussed by thousands of people I didn't know. I was pushed to become a mother, to have a child, a name, a birth, a grave, painful memories and endless shame.

Part of me is glad I went through what I did. It opened up a conversation in my country and shone a light on other people's situations as well. But it's interesting to wonder how my life would be now if things had been different.

This is my attempt to make sense of it all, no longer weighed down by guilt and shame. I am not Miss D any more. I'm Amy Dunne, and this is my story.

1

CHILDHOOD

know exactly where I was when my life changed for ever.

I was playing with my friends in a cul-de-sac near my home in County Kildare when my uncle Dennis pulled up alongside us in his car. My mother was in the passenger seat, making no effort to hide that she was crying. My little sister, Claire, was in the back. I was 12 years old.

My uncle rolled down the window. 'Come on, Amy, love,' he said. 'We have to go!' I was confused – Uncle Dennis didn't live near us. Even though I was very fond of him, we didn't see him a lot. I couldn't imagine where we could be going. But I did what I was told and waved goodbye to my surprised friends. I didn't know that was the last time we'd play together.

We had moved to the village of Sallins a couple of years earlier with my stepfather. Before that, we'd been living in

Clondalkin in Dublin. My mother had been dying to get out of the city. She and my stepdad bought a new house in an estate right beside one of the most beautiful parts of the Grand Canal.

I had spent the early years of my childhood in Jobstown in West Dublin with my mother and my sister, Sharon, who was eight years older than me. My dad wasn't around. Mam had met him after she moved to America in 1987 and lived for a time with her sister in Long Island in New York. The story she told me was that she was lost in the Bronx one day and a taxi driver, noticing her distress, pulled over to help her. He was a tall, brown-eyed, good-looking Italian American. My mam was a small, feisty, dark-eyed Dubliner, and from the moment they met, they fell in love. My dad had been in college, training to be a doctor, but he'd dropped out and was planning to move to San Francisco to be in a rock band. He wrote songs for my mam, who was bowled over by him.

They were dating for more than a year before Mam had to return home. She flew back to Dublin and thought the nausea and tiredness she was suffering from were caused by jet lag. In fact, she was in the early stages of pregnancy with me.

When I was born, my dad flew over to see us both. There's a photograph of him lying on the floor playing with me as a little baby. He looks every inch the bad-boy rock musician, with his long, flowing dark hair, sleeveless T-shirt and jeans. You can even see an electric guitar on the floor beside him.

He stayed with us for a while in my mother's little house in Jobstown. I don't know how long he had originally intended to stay in Ireland for. But the relationship ended suddenly when my mother found methadone in the fridge one morning and realised the extent of his drug addiction. That was the last time we were to see each other for almost three decades. My mother didn't tell me until much later why she had kicked him out, and for many years I blamed her unfairly for selfishly depriving me of a dad and of what I considered to be a 'normal' family. I didn't think about how tough it must have been for her. She'd had Sharon when she was 19, and she was almost 28 years old when I was born. After my dad went back to the States, she was left to bring up two kids on her own.

My dad's family stayed in contact with us, and over the years I got lots of letters and parcels from America. They were never directly from my dad but were sent from my uncle Frank and aunt Cathy, or from my granny Rafaella. They would send me dollars, beautiful clothes you would never find in Ireland and plenty of fabulous Barbie dolls to add to my collection. My favourite was a dark-skinned Barbie wearing a bright-yellow builder's outfit and matching hat. None of my friends had one like her and I adored her.

My mam was artistic and creative in her own way. She moved from Rathfarnham to Jobstown when I was born, and when I was young she worked as a community arts coordinator. The woman I remember from my childhood was a wild, waistcoat-wearing hippie with a paintbrush. She became involved in the arts through art therapy classes in a centre near our home that specialised in counselling and holistic treatments for local people. Her experience in this centre, Kiltalown House, led to her becoming one of the founder members of a group called Tallaght New Opportunities for Women, or Tallaght NOW. Among the others involved in the group was community activist Katherine Zappone, who later became a government minister and a campaigner for changing abortion legislation.

Jobstown was part of Tallaght, itself a huge suburb on the western outskirts of Dublin. When officials were planning it back in the 1970s, the intention was to create a new town to provide much needed housing and jobs. In the early 1990s, however, the area was suffering from high levels of unemployment and severe social problems. The growing population in sprawling new housing estates had very few facilities. Tallaght NOW was given funding to get local women back into the workforce and into education.

My mam was passionate about her work. The group started off with around three local women and grew until they had workers in 12 different parts of Tallaght. They helped hundreds of women to retrain, go back to school or set up their own businesses. Their first priority was to provide childcare for the women who needed it. Crèches were arranged, and many of the women set up their own community crèches after receiving training under the scheme.

Mam and her arts groups worked in schools, with early school-leavers and with local community groups, encouraging activities such as costume design, mask making and prop building, as well as organising parades where the young people could show off their skills. She also taught arts and crafts to women and children with special needs.

Our own house was overflowing with artwork. The kitchen table was always covered in paper and paints, crayons and markers. Mam loved making sculptures out of papier mâché in particular. On winter evenings, she lit the fire, and we sat in the cosy kitchen working together. Sharon was getting older and becoming much less interested in doing arts and crafts with her mam. But I loved it. We covered balloons with newspaper and water and formed strange creatures and elaborate masks. Mam had cupboards full of supplies – paints in dozens of colours and boxes full of glittery ribbons, googly eyes, feathers, fabric and sequins. She gave me glue and told me to decorate my creations in whatever way I wanted. She encouraged me to express myself and never lost her temper, no matter how much of a mess I made. One afternoon, she decided the kitchen itself was too boring and needed brightening up. She painted all the cupboards blue and decorated them with golden stencils of the sun. I thought it was the most beautiful room I'd ever seen! At home with Mam, I felt warm, happy, content and utterly safe. There was no badness. I felt totally loved.

My first appearance in a newspaper was thanks to one of Mam's projects. A former farmhouse near Jobstown was being turned into an arts centre. To celebrate this, for some reason, there was a picture of me, in the local newspaper, dressed up as a bumblebee alongside actress Brenda Fricker.

Through her work, my mother got involved with the Macnas street-theatre company in Galway. Members of Macnas came to Tallaght to help the women Mam worked with make huge dragonflies for parades in Galway, France and even China. She helped to establish a project where community groups from all over Ireland set up mini versions of the Macnas group. They travelled to each other's areas and to Galway to learn from one another and bring their skills back to their local communities.

My mam worked with Macnas for around three years, and I loved going to Galway with her for the arts festival every year. Mam, Sharon and I travelled to the West on the bus. If we were lucky, our first stop after getting off in Eyre Square would be at Supermac's for burgers and chips. Then we'd head to our bed and breakfast in nearby Salthill.

Macnas organised the accommodation, run by a young couple called Eileen and Dieter. Our first year staying with them coincided with their honeymoon, which they had decided to spend taking in guests in their new venture.

Eileen and Dieter became like family to us. We spent mornings collecting eggs from their chickens, as well as fruit and vegetables in the garden for our meals. For breakfast I drank freshly squeezed juice and sprinkled chopped chives from the herb garden on my scrambled eggs. We fed their fish and watered the tall sunflowers in their garden before heading off to the local community centre or parish hall to work on building floats and costumes.

Mam was involved in planning some of the performances. Sharon was taken off with a group of other teenagers to do workshops in performing and costume making. We younger children had group leaders to help us with our own activities. One year, I remember being surrounded by older children dressed as bluebells. They were carrying these exquisite, intricately designed flowers, four times my height. There was a golden sun, flanked by colourful dragonflies, and I was spinning around in my own custom-made costume – a giant pair of blue dungarees, turning me into a sweet baby bluebell.

On another occasion, I remember an elaborate float featuring a castle and, somehow, a waterfall with real water! A little girl, not much older than me, got to sit near the waterfall on a throne, wearing a golden crown. I loved dressing up and wearing costumes, but I was a frog that year, and I was not happy. While the princess was driven along on her colourful float, I had to hop along behind with all the other frogs. Worst of all, rumour had it that the children on the floats were going to get a bag of jellies each, while those of us on the ground would not. That was it for me. During rehearsals down by the river, I threw a spectacular tantrum. As Mam tried to bribe and cajole me to keep going, a newspaper photographer captured the moment, and I appeared in the paper the next day with the caption 'Stage fright at frog march'.

One evening when I was around five years old, Mam decided we should all go to the amusement arcade in Salthill after a long day of rehearsing. As a treat, she gave us cups of pennies to use in the machines. My favourite machine was the one where you tried to get a pile of coins to spill over the edge. I put my pennies in and that evening I finally got lucky! The coins poured out and I was richer than I had ever been in my life. Mam brought me to the souvenir shop next door to spend some of my winnings. I bought pencils, fridge magnets and sweets for my friends in Dublin. I let Mam spend the rest on bags of chips, drenched in vinegar, for the three of us. We ate them walking along the promenade, laughing and chatting as the sun went down.

Mam brought a bit of Macnas back to Tallaght with her in the form of a huge parade at the county council offices beside the shopping centre. Local kids made daisies as high as the Galway bluebells. There were marching bands and samba beats.

My mam was quite a spiritual person. I remember her praying, and she often brought me to light candles in the local church, but organised religion wasn't really part of our lives. Although we were technically Catholics, we said our prayers privately and didn't go to mass regularly, except at Christmas and Easter. I made my first holy communion when I was seven years old, but my most vivid memory of that day is throwing up shortly after receiving communion, and I refused to take it ever again! I believed in a kind, grandfather-like God. But from a very young age, I wasn't keen on the many rules and regulations that seemed to me to be part of being a Catholic.

It was Mam I worshipped. She meant everything to me as a child – too much, maybe. Sharon, like most young teenagers, was more interested in having fun with her friends than hanging out at home. I was my mam's little buddy. Everything she did, everywhere she went, I wanted to be there with her, stuck to her hip. I didn't want to stay in school without her and mitched off to be with her. Once a neighbour found me on the street, preparing to cross a busy road, determined to head back home to my mother. Mam was very upset with the school and gave them an earful, but it wasn't the last time I escaped. Another time, I told a teacher in the yard that my mam was collecting me outside the gate, and I got as far as the lollipop lady, who had to figure out what to do with me.

To me, Mam was the most beautiful woman on earth. I never remember her being angry, and she had an amazing ability to make everything fun. Our car was stolen when we lived in Jobstown, and so for a while we had to cycle everywhere. This wasn't a problem for Mam, though. She didn't moan or complain. On rainy mornings, she would tell me we were going on an adventure. She'd dress me up in all the right raingear, pop me onto the back of her bike and we'd set off in the lashing rain to school, with me holding on to her waist as tightly as I could. On other days, we walked for what seemed like hours through fields, Mam excitedly pointing out all the different plants and flowers and telling me their names. We may have been walking because we didn't have a car, but Mam always managed to make us see the adventure and excitement in everyday activities.

My aunties and uncles lived nearby, and we visited them often. Mam's friends were all mellow arty types like her, with flowing clothes and crazy, brightly coloured hair. Everyone was into expressing their emotions and living healthily. It was fun, and I was always the star of the show when we had visitors – I loved the attention. I'd be up on the table singing, dancing or telling jokes. I was full of confidence and rarely bold. Probably the most troublesome thing I did was talk to an imaginary 'man' at the end of my bed every night. Now, I think I must have been imagining I was talking to my granddad, who had died when I was a baby. Mam used to hear me laughing and chatting and had to come in to tell him to go away and encourage me to go to sleep.

My happiest childhood memories are from those days in Jobstown. Our house was on a corner site, surrounded by fields, and we sometimes found horses staring in at us from our front garden. We had a sheepdog called Sharky, and in the evenings, we would all snuggle up on the sofa with the dog and watch the soaps. I don't remember any troubles in our lives at all. There were rarely any men around. It was just us.

My stepdad first came on the scene when I was around five years old. It wasn't that I didn't like him – I just wasn't used to having a man in our lives. He was a businessman and travelled a lot for work. My mam decided it was time for her to settle down a bit, bring in a regular salary and 'be good'.

She got a job as a sales manager for a cleaning company. She wore suits and bought herself a big jeep. I went to a childminder after school. We had much more money, and she did a lot more of the things a 'normal' parent might do – more cleaning and cooking and having dinners ready in the evenings. But she didn't have as much time for me as she had before. I used to sleep in her bed; now I had to sleep on my own. Her routine completely changed and the arty, creative life we'd known all but disappeared. In my dramatic mind, my mam seemed to be wilting like a flower. To me, it was as if the colour faded out of our lives.

Mam and my stepdad bought a house together and we moved into a nice part of Clondalkin. I changed schools, settled well and made loads of friends. My stepdad had a son, two years younger than me, who stayed with us most weekends. I thought he was totally spoiled, but we got along well enough. He had every gadget and toy a boy could want, and his father adored him. Not long afterwards, my little sister, Claire, came along and was everyone's princess. Sharon was becoming a young adult. She started earning her own money and moved out of home. I felt like nobody's child.

To try to make sure I didn't feel too left out, I was spoiled as well. There was a trip to a toy shop almost every week, where I could pick out whatever I wanted. I was overjoyed when I was allowed to get the shiny pink Barbie jeep I'd had my heart set on for months. When I was around ten years old, I got a bright-yellow Discman on which I could play my favourite CDs. I loved B*Witched, the Spice Girls and the

Backstreet Boys, and I thought I was the coolest kid in town. I got my first mobile phone at the age of 11, because my stepbrother was getting one and I had to get one too. The only person who called me on my Nokia was my mother, and the only other thing I could do with it was play Snake, but I was thrilled with it.

We went on outings with my stepdad most weekends. We'd have a big breakfast at home before heading off to Blessington Lakes or Fort Lucan Adventure Playground or Clara Lara Funpark in Wicklow. It was always something fun and outdoorsy.

I didn't notice the problems between my mam and stepdad until long after they had started. I was a just a kid, and I was busy thinking about myself. I was too obsessed with my own jealousy about Mam not being around as much as I wanted to be aware of anything she was going through. As I got a bit older, I started to notice that my stepdad often came home late from work. I would hear arguments between them – they weren't making as much of an effort as they used to to keep the rows hidden from us. The arguments became more intense, and gradually I realised that everything was not OK in our previously perfect lives.

The idea was that the house in Kildare would be a fresh start for all of us. It was a brand-new house in a newly built estate. We had watched it being built, going on regular day trips to Sallins to see its progress, until finally the day came to make the move.

I found the change tough. It was made more difficult by my stepdad insisting I should wear a Dublin football jersey for my first day in my new school. That didn't go down too well with my Kildare classmates. But, at heart, I was a happy-go-lucky, fun-loving child and I found my feet quickly.

One of my favourite television programmes as a young child was *Rosie and Jim* – a show about two ragdolls who lived on a narrowboat. When we moved, it was as if I had been transported into their world. A short distance away from our estate were moorings for houseboats, just underneath a stone humpbacked bridge. I couldn't believe people actually lived in these crazy, colourful homes. I loved to watch from the bridge as the boats made their way slowly up and down the water. Or I'd sit for ages on the canal bank watching people going about their everyday lives on their floating houses.

Mam loved the outdoors and nature and encouraged me to spend as much time as possible outside. I loved playing by the water. Some of the older teenagers had built a treehouse right beside the canal, and when they weren't around, we younger kids would take over and hang out there.

The things we got up to would horrify parents now. One day we decided to make rafts out of some wooden pallets we found on the canal bank. A few of the older boys stuffed the pallets full of foam, then looked for volunteers to test them out. I was always up for an adventure, and I was the first to accept the challenge. I sat on the pallet while the others pushed me off the bank, everyone shouting and cheering when they realised our raft wasn't going to sink. I was cheering too, until I noticed I was in the middle of the canal between the two banks and didn't seem to be moving towards either one. After they stopped laughing, the others found a large stick to throw to me, which I managed to use as a paddle to steer myself back to shore.

We got plenty of use out of those rafts. We even tried fishing using sticks, string and a few worms dug up from the canal bank. Not surprisingly, we didn't catch very much. One afternoon, however, I saw a huge green–grey fish with silver spots floating along in the water just beside me. I scooped it out and my friends were stunned that I had managed to catch this amazing creature. The fact that it was already dead didn't really matter to us. Mam, however, was not so impressed when I got home and presented her with a foot-and-a-half-long rotting pike for our tea.

We played tip the can, chasing and innocent games of kiss-chase. I took up skateboarding and became a real tomboy for a while, skating along in my baggy clothes, until I realised I wasn't much good at it. I had piano lessons every Sunday morning. I tried dancing and karate before I found my real childhood passion: horse-riding.

My first lesson was unusual. The woman who ran the stables wasn't overly fond of children and certainly didn't believe in pandering to them. While I loved horses and had adored looking at pictures of them, I was petrified of the real animals. She sat me up immediately on a horse with no saddle and told me to hold on to the mane and get on with it. I survived five minutes of cantering bareback on this horse, clutching on to his mane for dear life. After that, there wasn't much about horses that could scare me.

Once a month, she took a few of us with her to the horse fair in Smithfield Square in Dublin. Her aim was to save some of the horses who had been badly treated. She would buy them and bring them back to Kildare, where we would help to clean them up and care for them. We brushed their manes and tails, fed them and cleaned out their stables. The horse I looked after most often was called Cara – I chose her because I knew her name meant 'friend' in Irish. She was a big, beautiful chestnut-coloured mare. I used to spend hours plaiting her mane, chatting away to her as I did so.

My mother had been worried about the bad influence of older teenagers and the growing prevalence of drugs in the areas around our home in Dublin. She was delighted and relieved that we were enjoying this safe, fun outdoorsy life.

Both she and my stepdad were working really hard in their jobs. We had what seemed like a lavish lifestyle in our new home, with lots of nice things. I suppose it was meant to make up for what was going on between them.

The day it all changed was 16 June 2002 – Father's Day. Ireland was also playing Spain in the World Cup. Mam had bought tickets for us all to watch the match and have something to eat in the local pub – a lovely place called the Bridgewater Inn, beside the canal. My mam hated football or any kind of sport, so this was a big gesture she was making for my stepdad as a surprise.

The first indication that something was wrong was that my stepdad didn't show up to the pub. It didn't bother me too much. I got to sit and chat with Mam, and I was excited to have a glass of Coke as a treat. But my mam looked distraught. We left before the match ended, and I went to play with my friends while my mother went home with my little sister. Apart from the fact that Mam was a bit upset, it was a normal enough Sunday, until that moment my uncle pulled up in the car.

Uncle Dennis was also my godfather, and I was excited to see him. I really wanted to believe him when he told me we were going on a little holiday. I tried to tell myself my mam's tears were just her being dramatic, but I knew in my heart something was very wrong. I didn't know then that there had been another huge row with my stepdad when she'd got home from the pub, and Mam had finally decided she'd had enough.

My uncle told me the name of the town we were going to. I couldn't pronounce it, and I didn't have a clue where it was or why we were going there. The car journey lasted for about an hour, and everyone was very quiet, apart from me. As per usual, I asked dozens of questions, but I didn't get any straight answers.

It was starting to get dark when we arrived in Drogheda. We drove into what appeared to me to be a large town, weaving in and out of side streets, turning the car around on numerous occasions, as my uncle asked Mam to repeat the address again and again. I heard them mention the word 'stables', which immediately sparked my interest. I allowed myself to hope we really were just going on a holiday after all and I was going to go horse-riding. Finally, we turned into a laneway and pulled up beside a grey and red-brick building with black wrought-iron gates set into a wide archway. My mam squeezed my hand as we approached the gates and rang the buzzer. 'It'll be all right, Amy,' she said. I didn't believe her.

The courtyard we were entering had indeed once housed a stables and a coach house, back in the late 19th century. There were no horses by the time we got there, though. It was part of the Drogheda Women's Refuge: our new home.

Behind the former stables was a tall, austere-looking red-brick building. It reminded me of a schoolhouse or a convent and it smelled as you'd expect – old and musty. My little sister and I were shooed upstairs, while my mam spoke to the women in charge.

We found ourselves in a large living room, with a television in one corner. Several women and one or two children were in the room, most watching the television. We shyly went over to join them. Claire, who was just three years old, refused to let go of my hand.

It seemed like some kind of secret society, where no men were allowed. I wasn't too upset to be there. The women were kind, and we found a playroom full of toys, which were a distraction. In any case, I was sure we would be staying for only a night or two at most.

My mam was given some food and night clothes for us. Holding on to the iron handrails, we climbed the steep staircase towards our bedroom on the top floor. It was a small room, around the size of the box room at our home in Sallins. I didn't yet know the lovely house near the water would never be my home again.

There was a window, a wardrobe and one set of bunkbeds in the room. On some nights, Mam would snuggle in with Claire while I slept on my own up on the top bunk. Sometimes

I'd sleep with Claire while Mam slept on her own. Claire cried every single night. She was only three years old. She missed her daddy and she missed Sharky. I cuddled her and tried to comfort her and told her we were on a little holiday, convincing her we were staying in Princess Fiona's house, just like in her favourite movie, *Shrek*. But there were nights when I also cried myself to sleep, and in the bunk above me I'd hear my mam trying to muffle the sound of her own sobs.

We shared a bathroom, kitchen and sitting room with other families. I hated sharing the bathroom. I was 12 years old and starting to become sensitive about my appearance and my personal hygiene. I hated having to wash myself or use the shower there, as I had no slippers or flip-flops. All my clothes, everything I owned, had been left behind in Kildare. It made me feel gross to walk on the bare tiles after seeing so many other people go in and out of the same room.

After a few days, I was brought to a room downstairs by one of the women in charge of the refuge. She showed me piles of second-hand clothes, all in my size, and told me to pick some out for myself. I was used to having a lot of material things, but we had left Kildare with only the shorts and T-shirt I had been dressed in, so I really appreciated getting these clothes. I had always loved picking out outfits, and this was almost as good as going shopping. I scooped up armfuls of tops, leggings and jeans and went back to my room to try them on. It was a real novelty. My mam noticed how much the clothes cheered me up and promised she would buy me a new jacket as soon as she could. A few weeks later, she kept her promise, bringing me to a quirky little shop across the road from the refuge. I chose a long denim jacket with blue fur all around it. I lived in that jacket every day and thought I looked like a model. It had to be peeled off me to get it washed, but I had very little else and it meant a lot to me.

The sitting room was homely and cosy when no one else was around, but that didn't happen often. Usually there would be at least one other family in the room, and it used to drive me mad, as we'd have to go through a process of negotiating and bargaining to get to watch our favourite television programmes.

The upheaval of the move meant that I missed a couple of days of school. As soon as she could, Mam packed me off to the nearest primary school, but I lasted one day and refused to go back. I just couldn't do it – I felt uncomfortable and weird. It was an all-girls school and I had never been to a school like that before. I was in sixth class – my last year in primary school. With less than two weeks of the school year left, no one was interested in getting to know the new girl.

By now I was beginning to realise this was more than just a holiday. We'd never been on a holiday before where I had been forced to go to school. I cried so much that my mam felt bad for me and came up with a new plan. She organised for me to stay with a friend in Sallins and finish my last week of primary school education there. I stuck it out for the little time there was left, but everything was different. I was mortified trying to explain to my friends why I had left so suddenly and where I was now living. I wanted to get back to my mam as quickly as possible.

To pass the time at the refuge, I helped out in the playroom, minding my sister and the other younger kids. I loved this work. My experience travelling around the arts workshops with my mam, as well as my love of drama, meant I found it easy to entertain the little kids and they loved me. The families in the refuge were from all kinds of backgrounds. Some were escaping from addiction issues or from domestic violence, and others simply had nowhere else to go. I got to know boys and girls from different walks of life who hadn't had the kind of happy childhood I had been lucky enough to enjoy for so long. I did arts and crafts with them, the way my mam had shown me; I played games and put on shows. I think the women at the refuge encouraged me to look after the younger kids in an effort to make me feel needed. When I was with them, I didn't feel sorry for myself: I believed I was helping others. So many children there were in a worse position than I was, with parents who couldn't mind them.

I loved playing with the four- and five-year-olds, trying to make them smile and laugh.

Mam started to make friends with the other mothers, and they would sit around chatting in the evenings. In my memory, she didn't drink at all at that time. Some of the younger women would sometimes sneak in bottles of alcohol and have a few drinks, especially on weekend nights. Even though Mam wasn't involved, this still made me feel uncomfortable.

I wondered when we were going to go home and tried to find out from Mam what was happening. But I couldn't get a straight answer out of her. She was so broken herself that she didn't recognise how anxious and lonely I was becoming. She had too much of her own stuff to deal with.

The refuge was a safe place for us – it was warm and welcoming, and the people were supportive and kind. But it was not where we should have been. My sense of security and safety had taken a huge knock. I had always felt safe as long as I was with my mam; now I didn't know what the future had in store. I thought we'd be there for a couple of weeks at most. Instead, we stayed for six months.

2

RUNNING WILD

'This is it!' my mam told us proudly, pointing through the trees. 'Our new place!' She was delighted and so excited. She'd heard about this house in the refuge. With some help, she had been able to put together the deposit for the landlord. She had left her job when we left Sallins, and we were relying on the little savings she had. Now, after six months of living in a tiny box room, we were finally moving into our own home.

If the sun was shining, and you looked in a certain direction, it was easy to share my mother's enthusiasm. We were back beside the water, this time on the banks of the River Boyne, which was across the road from us. Our new home was one of a row of six, surrounded by large gardens. They were built along a wide avenue, overhung by trees, leading off towards the grounds of Greenhills school, the local convent secondary school. On the other side of the avenue was a football field, and a little further along there was even a tennis court! My mam must have hoped she had found another perfect rural location in which she could bring up her children.

Just one glance in the opposite direction, however, and the reality of the situation became clear. We were on the grounds of a huge factory, just outside the town. Premier Periclase had been part of the Drogheda landscape since before I was born. The factory made products used in the steel and cement industries, and its rusty chimney towered over the site. The houses had originally been home to some of the workers but were now rented out privately. Only three of the six, including ours, were occupied – the others were derelict. My mam, my little sister and I were all standing in what was the workers' car park, our bags containing the few belongings we had at our feet. It was dusk, the factory was quiet and the whole place had an eerie atmosphere.

'Come on!' shouted Mam, waving the keys at me, trying to make this another one of our fun adventures. We picked up our bags and followed her in. Her excitement was contagious, and I tried my best to see the place through her eyes. A woman who worked at the refuge lived in one of the other occupied houses at the end of the row. She was the one who had told Mam this place was available, and Mam had jumped at the chance to get out. This place was much bigger than anywhere we had previously lived. We had been sharing bunkbeds for six months: now we would each have our own bedroom.

That was where my enthusiasm ended, though, despite Mam's best efforts. The house was dark and old fashioned, with all kinds of nooks and crannies. The gloomy hallway led into a vast but dated kitchen. Beside it was a room that looked like my idea of a scullery – a narrow room containing a long sink. Beyond that was a boiler room and a utility room, which my mam planned to turn into an artist's studio. At the back of the house was a long-neglected conservatory with vines growing through the panes of glass in the roof. Upstairs were our bedrooms and a cold bathroom that provided a home for spiders the size of my hand. There were gaps in the floorboards, and I was certain I could hear a scurrying sound beneath my feet. My mother told me I was being dramatic, as per usual. 'Don't worry, Amy,' she said, 'it'll be perfect.'

Mam certainly did her best to make it a home for us. Over the following weeks and months, she painted walls, filled holes, bought new carpets and gave us the best bedrooms we could have dreamed of. My room was painted purple with silver and purple stickers on the walls. I had one of those beds with a pull-out desk and shelves underneath it, something I had always wanted. My little sister's room had a Winnie-the-Pooh theme, and her bed even had a slide!

We got tennis rackets and practised hitting the ball on

the moss-covered court outside. Every Sunday we watched football matches on the playing field opposite our front garden. Those Sunday-morning matches were the only time anyone other than ourselves or the workers visited the area.

The factory was more than two kilometres from the town. In the mornings, I made my way through the woods between the end of the avenue and the adjoining convent to catch a bus to my own school. In the dark winter evenings, if I wasn't getting a lift, I was faced with the choice of making my way back through the dark and dense woodland into the factory grounds or walking the almost equally lonely road from the town, with the River Boyne on one side and a high stone wall on the other.

A girl around my age lived in one of the other occupied houses, and after a few weeks, I discovered we could make our way to each other's gardens through a tunnel in the trees. It was just as well I had her to play with, as other children were freaked out by the place. No one ever wanted to stay in the house too long. They were always eager to get home before it got dark and never wanted to stay the night.

When evening came and the machinery fell silent, there were no lights at all outside. All we could see from the front windows of the house was darkness, the grey shapes of the factory buildings looming in the background. Even in daylight it looked like one of the factories described in the 19th-century novels I had to study in English class. During the day, the noise from the factory was constantly in the background. Every so often the noise would continue through the night, and we would wake up to find our car windows covered in thick dust.

The move did bring us some happiness, though. One afternoon, not long after we'd moved in, I arrived home from school to be greeted by a black-and-white ball of craziness. We'd left Sharky back in Sallins with my stepdad. Now we were out of the refuge, it meant she could live with us again.

Mam wasted no time transforming the utility room at the far end of the house into the studio she had planned. She began making candles and stained-glass candle holders to sell at the market in town. On the rare days when friends came over, they were fascinated by her work – no other mother was doing this kind of thing. They loved it even more when she encouraged us to join in. She would get us to pour wax into moulds and to design our own candle holders. But as time went by, she began to spend more and more time working away in this room on her own. It meant that she had peace and quiet but also that she could hide away from us. Getting to the studio from the other side of the house meant walking through the hallway, past the dark staircase, and it terrified me. I became scared to look out the windows, convinced the whole place was haunted.

I understand why Mam wanted to have a proper home for her children, as any parent would. She had brought us to Drogheda in the first place in a panic. Anxious to get out of her relationship and desperate to provide us with a roof over our heads, she had headed for the first place that had a space for us. She was delighted to be able to finally leave the refuge and to have somewhere we could call our own. This new house, however, was probably in the very worst part of Drogheda we could have chosen. We didn't know anyone in the area and there wasn't much opportunity to make friends living away from everything and everybody. My mam felt isolated and lonely, and this is when I think many of our most serious problems began. It was around this time that she started suffering from what I now believe was depression. I wouldn't have known to call it that in those days. All I knew was that she was often sad and stressed. I was becoming a teenager and she was suffering. It was not a good combination.

At first, she tried to make the best of our situation. She got a little bit of money from the sale of a property in Dublin, and once a month we would take a trip into the town centre. We loved those trips. She would buy us our favourite magazines, as well as ice cream and treats, and sometimes she'd pick up a bottle of champagne or sparkling wine for herself. We'd snuggle up at home, Mam with her glass of bubbles, us with our treats and our magazines. Soon the trips started happening more regularly. We'd go into town for 'treats' every fortnight, then every week. Mam, who had never really been much of a drinker, was drinking almost all the time.

It started to affect all aspects of our lives. In the mornings, Mam sometimes wouldn't get out of bed. There would be nothing for lunch and no clean school uniforms in the house. On days when she was due to pick me up from school, she would be an hour late or she'd forget completely. One evening, I trekked home through the woods to find her lying on the couch, incapable of getting up. Her voice sounded strange: slurry and distant. She told me she was going to drive to the shops to get dinner. I grabbed the car keys and refused to give them back to her. I was scared. This was not the mother I knew. She didn't even sound like herself.

When I was little, Mam often told me that we'd run away and live in Galway with the theatre group for ever. Now she told me she was going to leave me and run away with my little sister instead. I knew she didn't really mean it, but I was devastated by her words. I didn't know anyone in the town who could help me, and even if I had, I would have been too embarrassed to admit what was going on, so I put up with our situation in silence for a long time. Mam was my idol, and she was falling apart.

❖

Starting secondary school in a new town was difficult, even more so because of what was going on at home. On my very first day, the teacher asked if there was any student in the classroom who didn't know anyone else at all. I put up my hand and looked around to see that mine was the only hand raised. I felt like an alien, and for a while the others treated me like one. Being seen as a 'Dub' didn't help. But I was used to being the new girl. I had a flair for drama and enjoyed making people laugh, so I made one or two good friends in the first weeks. Having friends to talk to kept me going for a while and allowed me to ignore everything else that was happening. I knew what a normal, healthy family life looked like, and I knew what was going on in my home didn't fit that picture. I didn't want anyone else to find out about it.

I tried to get away from my house as much as possible. I made one friend who lived in a big bungalow in the countryside. When I went over to her house, we played out in the fields, running around hay bales or scaring the cows. Relations between my stepdad and my mother had improved, and he had started taking Claire to stay with him a lot more. I tagged along with them as much as I could, while wishing my own father was around too.

I was a smart kid. In my first two years in secondary school, I was often called a 'swot' because I always had my hand up. I was made class president two years in a row because the other kids knew I wouldn't be shy about asking questions. My teachers probably felt I asked too many!

I loved Irish and maths in particular, but there was one subject I didn't do well in. After the incident with the communion bread back in primary school, I had lost interest in religion. In my first year of religion class in my new secondary school, I told the teacher I did not want to read the Bible. I just didn't believe the stories and I had lots of questions about the religion I had been brought up in. I believed in God. I thought of him as a sort of kindly figure who loved people unconditionally. But I couldn't buy into all the things that were supposed to have happened according to the Bible. I was also confused about the rules and regulations. I didn't think it was fair, for example, that priests couldn't be in a relationship. I didn't have any strong views on issues like abortion, though. I don't remember that being something that was ever mentioned, let alone discussed, until I was around 15 or 16 years old.

I knew from what my mam had told me, and from some of the letters I had received from my dad's family in America, that my dad was interested in Buddhism, so I became intrigued by that for a while. I wanted to believe there was someone or something watching over me, especially as life became more difficult. I prayed a lot and sometimes I felt only God could have saved me or my mam from situations in which we could have been harmed. But as I got older, it seemed the more I prayed, the worse things got.

A number of events finally sparked our departure from the factory grounds. First of all, Sharky went missing. We spent the evening frantically searching for her in the overgrown fields all around the houses. We found her after a few hours in the field furthest from the factory, covered in melted tar. We cleaned her up and got her checked out. She seemed fine, but from then on, we worried every time she escaped from the garden.

Not long afterwards, it turned out that the scurrying I'd thought I heard under the floorboards when we moved in was not, in fact, a figment of my overactive imagination. One morning, I came downstairs for breakfast to find a large rat had eaten its way through the box of cornflakes in the kitchen press. I became hyper-aware of every little noise, and I was convinced there were hordes of rats under the houses. Given that we were just across the road from the river, my fears were probably based in reality. Rat poison was laid all around the car park and the grounds surrounding the houses. Within a couple of days, Sharky had vanished again. This time we couldn't find her, no matter how hard we looked. My mam believed she must have eaten poison and taken herself off somewhere to die. That was the final straw for all of us. Even my mother couldn't put a brave face on Sharky's disappearance and probable death, and she started looking for somewhere else to rent.

We moved to a new estate, much nearer to my school. We had built up our lives again since our arrival at the women's refuge, and this time we arrived at our new home with suitcases and a small vanload of furniture.

It was a lovely house in a good area. It now took just minutes to get to class, and I didn't have to walk through a dark forest along the way. But I found it hard to settle. I was still ashamed that we were renting and that I didn't have a dad. It seemed to me that all my classmates came from perfect families, with a mam and a dad, all happy and smiling. My mam didn't have a partner and I felt I didn't fit in. I knew Mam was really trying hard to make our lives better and to stay away from drink, but she was still struggling. Part of the problem was that she was in denial about the extent of our problems, and she refused to admit she needed help. Although I tried to discuss it with her when we were at home, I didn't want to admit outside the house that anything was wrong. Once again, I was obsessed with keeping up appearances and not letting people see what was really going on. It was, however, a lot easier to keep up the pretence now that we lived in what I considered to be a 'normal' house in a 'normal' area. I took more care than ever about the way I looked. Everything about me had to be perfect – from my matching hair bobbins to my spotless school uniform and colourful clothes. I hoped no one would suspect anything.

I have always used my appearance to express myself and to hide the imperfections in my life. I had a real interest in clothes and in dressing up while I was growing up, and I dressed differently to lots of the other kids. When I was very young, Mam had the money to encourage me. She herself loved bright multicoloured clothes – waistcoats and flowing skirts. When I wasn't dressed up in some crazy outfit for a costume or a parade, she liked dressing me in big fluffy dresses, like a little doll. As I got older, I continued to treat my clothes as costumes. There are photographs of me wearing pink dungarees, and one of my favourite outfits was a pink miniskirt and a pink satin bomber jacket with fur all around the hood. I liked to wear ra-ra skirts with my favourite crushed velvet boots and the denim jacket Mam had bought me after we arrived in the refuge. On another day, I could choose to wear a shirt and trousers, or a pair of combats and a belly top. My clothes gave me the confidence to face the very different world I had found myself in since leaving Kildare.

I had no concept of trying to look 'sexy' or 'attractive' to boys in these outfits, even as I turned into a teenager. I still secretly played with my beloved Barbie dolls. I dressed them up in their own fancy outfits and drove them around my bedroom in their lovely pink jeep. Really, all I was trying to do was look as perfect and pretty as my dolls.

My efforts began to backfire, though, particularly in school. One of my teachers, seeing me ready for PE class in my bright-blue velour tracksuit, jokingly called me 'Aqua Barbie'. He didn't mean any harm at all. But among some of my classmates, the name stuck and was later used against me.

My mam, despite all that was going on, tried to ensure as much as she could that I always had money for school trips or anything else I needed. She had bought me all the gear I needed for my horse-riding classes back in Sallins – the jacket, the boots and the jodhpurs. In Drogheda, she tried to enrol me in a horse-riding camp, hoping I'd rediscover my love of horses and that it would keep me out of trouble. But I told her I didn't want to do it. I was more interested in hanging around with friends.

I was desperate to fit in with the other girls and boys in my class. It was the end of second year, we were all 14 and 15 years old and it seemed as if everyone was boasting about having sex and losing their virginity. I thought everyone else had done it and I decided I'd better do it too. There was an older boy who was showing some interest in me. He had a moped and lots of the girls fancied him. I decided he'd be the boy I'd lose my virginity to. It was a horrible experience for me, but he boasted about it to his friends, and soon practically the whole school knew. It was a stupid thing to have done. Instead of helping me to fit in, it marked the start of the bullying that intensified during the following months.

When my mam found out, she was livid. The following day, she headed up to the school just in time to meet my little 'boyfriend' along the road. She whacked him over the head with his own schoolbag and told him to stay away from me. She wanted to kill him – I was still her little girl. I was mortified, of course, but inside, I was also quite proud of her and glad that she obviously still cared so much about me. I had become used to seeing my mam as someone who was weak, but I saw strength in her reaction to the boy – in my eyes it was like something a father would do. The boy didn't come near me again after that.

Our new home, at the back of a recently built estate, faced on to a green area. There was a low enough wall separating our estate from a neighbouring housing development. In the summer of 2004, a group of boys who lived nearby started hopping over this wall and hanging out on the green area, drinking, smoking and generally messing around. My mam and the other neighbours were not happy about the boys' behaviour or their attitude, but there was nothing they could do about them gathering in a public space. If there was any sign they might get into trouble, or if the Gardaí were called, the boys would just hop back over the wall and run off through the surrounding fields.

They weren't much older than I was, and it didn't take them long to notice me, as I walked around in my boots and flouncy skirts. They whistled and shouted and tried to talk to me. At first, I ignored them. After all, these were clearly 'bad boys'. But I was bored, a bit lonely and very flattered. I began chatting with them from my bedroom window at the front of the house. After a while, I plucked up the courage to join them on the green. Sometimes I jumped over the wall with them and headed to the fields a bit further away to avoid my angry neighbours. Mam didn't always notice when I wasn't at home, so I stayed out later and later. I started to rebel.

When I got to know them, I couldn't understand why the adults didn't like these boys. I didn't really have that many close friends at school any more, and I felt safer and happier with these guys than with anyone else. I didn't see any badness in them. While other people thought they were brats and delinquents, to me they were just my pals.

The neighbours complained to my mother that I was encouraging the boys to keep hanging around. For a while, Mam tried to pay more attention to what I was doing but by now I had no respect for her or for her authority. I was on a mission to defy her. When she locked my bedroom door at night, I climbed out my window and slid down to the ground before running off with my new friends. This happened almost every night. Occasionally, some of the older boys turned up in cars, screeching around the estate, doing doughnuts and skids, causing mayhem. I'd jump into a car, followed by Mam chasing out of the house after me, screaming my name. I didn't care. I came and went as I wanted.

When I returned to school after the summer holidays, everything was different. Word of my new friends got around, and some of the other kids let me know exactly what they thought of them and of me. I heard the names 'tramp', 'slut' and 'Barbie doll'. There were threats that I'd be beaten up and comments that I deserved to die.

The bullying devastated me, but outwardly, I pretended to be tough and decided to play up to my new bad-girl image instead of rejecting it.

I met my first real boyfriend on New Year's Eve 2004. My friend and I were hanging around the estate, looking for a bit of craic. More specifically, we were looking for someone who would buy us alcohol. One of the boys, who was slightly older than us, offered to buy us drink and invited us to a party later that night.

The party wasn't much of a celebration. A group of us ended up sitting around in a room in this guy's house drinking the green Aftershock he had bought for us earlier. After a while, I noticed another older boy staring over at me. He must have stared for about an hour before he finally started talking to me. It was pretty clear he liked me, but he also gave the impression he wasn't too bothered whether I was interested in him or not. For a needy, hormonal teenage girl, that was a lethal combination. I was hooked.

He asked me if I liked any of the other boys there, before kissing me. From that moment on, we were inseparable. He was skinny and not much taller than I was, but he had a swagger about him. He threatened to kill anyone who came near me, and I was wowed by his 'tough guy' attitude. Threatening people wasn't in my nature, and I didn't like it when he did it. But part of me was flattered that he felt so strongly about me and wanted, as I saw it, to look after me. I loved the security he gave me. He was also the only man I had in my life.

His own life wasn't perfect either. He had lost his father in a horrific car crash when he was only nine years old. The death left his mother alone with five young children, of whom my boyfriend was the eldest. Looking back, I can see we were both damaged and trying to save each other.

He had given up on school a few years previously. He and his friends used to sleep during the day and come out at night. I climbed out my bedroom window every evening to meet him – any chance we got, we were together. We walked around the estates, holding hands until we got to our favourite spot – a hill near the Ramparts, overlooking the river.

You could see everything from there – the cathedral spire, the bridge over the Boyne and, if you stretched really hard, over the treetops you could make out the factory chimney beside my former home further down the river. The trees and thick shrubbery provided shelter and prevented us from being seen. It was also right above the local McDonald's, where I could nip in to buy Cokes or use the toilet. We'd sit among the trees, out of sight, with a bottle of Coke and a naggin of vodka, when we could afford it, talking, chilling out and messing around. There was a complete sense of freedom there, away from everyone else.

In April 2005, four months after we got together, I turned 15. My boyfriend turned up to meet me that night with a huge parcel. Inside were a pair of boots I'd been admiring for ages and a bottle of Chupa Chups perfume. I was absolutely thrilled with the presents and with him. I didn't know then that his mother was the one who had gone out to get the gifts. I was just overwhelmed that I had someone who cared so much about me.

The bullying I was suffering had intensified during the school year and I'd been attending classes less and less. I was not the only one attracted by my boyfriend's innocent face and bad-boy personality, and some of the attention I was getting was fuelled by jealousy. One day, I was cornered on my way into school by a group of girls who pushed me into the railings, calling me a slut and a slag. It was very intimidating, but I managed to escape and ran to the school yard, sobbing.

The teacher on yard duty was not sympathetic. She told me to get on with it and get myself to class. My best friend was busy, talking to a gang of boys. I felt I'd lost all my friends and that everyone was talking about me. I turned around and fled out of the gates.

I was due to sit my Junior Certificate examinations in the school that summer. I tried to go back. I knew I should sit the exams. Most mornings, however, I panicked and couldn't force myself to go in. On the days when I made it as far as the exam hall, I lasted about an hour before giving up and running home. I refused point blank to go back to school the following September, despite my mam's best efforts to make me.

My relationship with Mam was getting worse. Now, of course, I can see how difficult I must have been to manage. If my own child did half of the things I did back then, I'd have him locked up in boarding school in a flash! I was cheeky, I wouldn't go to school, I demanded money whenever I needed it, and I did whatever I wanted whenever I chose. Mam tried to keep me under control and grounded me practically every week, but I'd just sneak back out again, and she would never be able to find me in our secret spot. There was no holding me down.

This was a time when I was at my wildest and my mam was at her lowest. She took to the bottle a bit more as I took to the streets. She started to go out drinking herself, and sometimes she wouldn't come back for hours. I was scared that she wouldn't come back at all – that she'd fall or be mugged, or worse.

It was clear to everyone, including my mother, that this situation couldn't go on. She decided to ask for help and voluntarily put me into the care of social workers. My mother said afterwards she felt relieved when she made that decision. She felt she wasn't doing a good enough job as a mother and couldn't give me the structure and discipline I needed. Her plan was that she would get help and dry out while I was being minded in a stable family home. She thought I'd have regular, healthy meals, that I'd get back to school and be home every night by eight. It didn't quite work out like that.

Over the following two years, I ended up in two foster-care placements as well as two bed and breakfasts, in between months of living with my mam in various rented accommodation all around Drogheda. On one occasion we were given a room in a hostel for the homeless, after my mother's landlord changed the locks on the house. I lost everything that time. We never got back into that house, and I didn't get any of my clothes back. I spent days wearing the same orange gypsy skirt, leggings and flip-flops. This would normally have bothered me, but I was so worried about my mother at the time that, for once, I didn't care what I looked like.

A pattern developed. Every time my mam got into difficulty and asked for help, I'd be taken away from her and put into care. Then she would recover a little, she'd get settled, I'd go back, and we'd start all over again. The fact that most of the placements I was put in were voluntary didn't mean anything to me. All I knew was that I was being taken away from my family and put somewhere I didn't want to be, with people who were strangers to me. I felt like an inconvenience to everyone and that I was someone no one wanted to have around.

I started attending the Youthreach programme in the town, for early school leavers. And I was assigned a social worker called Martina who was like a 'buddy' to me. She would try to take the pressure off my mam and give me some kind of normal life by bringing me out for a few hours every week or so. She was in her late twenties or early thirties and didn't have children of her own, so she was more like another big sister to me. My own big sister, Sharon, was working and off living her own life by then, while my little sister Claire stayed more often with her dad.

I didn't really confide in Martina or have deep conversations with her, but she gave me a lovely escape from my reality for a few hours. We went to Funtasia, the amusement park in Drogheda, or we'd go to the cinema or out for lunch. She was kind, friendly and giddy – we had great chats and just had fun. It was nice to forget about the serious problems at home, even for a little while. I didn't have aunties or uncles or any other adults I was close to in Drogheda, so I liked having someone to mind me, even if she was being paid to do it.

Mam had been trying to persuade me to keep up my schooling, but I rarely went to my Youthreach classes. When I turned 16, in 2006, I got a job in the local Kentucky Fried Chicken. Work has always been important to me. I haven't had a long period of being without a job since I was 12 years old, and there have been times I've worked two jobs to support myself. A friend of Mam's gave me my first job, selling strawberries in the market in Drogheda on Saturdays. Sometimes, my friend and I were sent to sell them on the side of the road. Spending 10 hours on the side of the motorway with no food and no access to toilets wasn't fun, but I was determined to earn money and didn't complain. I took a strawberry from every punnet to keep myself going and went to the toilet in a ditch if I had to. I moved on to working in a local newsagent's when I was 13. The job in KFC was my first full-time role and meant I could afford to look after myself. Frying chicken doesn't sound glamorous, but to me, it meant freedom. I worked on the till and had more money in my pocket than I'd ever had in my life. The people I worked with became my friends and like a second family to me.

We were working in a new outlet in the town, getting it ready to open. I didn't have as much time for my boyfriend, and being around a more mature bunch of people made me question what I was doing with my own life. Some of the people I worked with had aspirations to go to college or get a qualification. They were earning a living and using their wages to enjoy themselves.

I got notions myself and decided to buy a moped from one of the guys in work. It was a black and red Gilera scooter that looked amazing, even if it was a bit too big for me to handle. At the beginning, it fell over every time I stopped, and it was difficult for someone as small as me to pick it back up again. Gradually, I got the hang of it, and I became a familiar sight around the area, zipping to work and back in my bright-pink combats. I started to gain confidence as well as a new perspective on life.

My mother and I were still fighting. I felt she was being unfair because, for once, I wasn't running wild – I was working every waking hour. Nevertheless, one of our frequent arguments ended with her throwing my stuff out on the footpath and telling me not to come back. That particular time, I decided to sort myself out before the social workers got involved and I went to find myself somewhere to live. I pretended to a local woman that I was 18, not 16, and managed to rent a room. For a few weeks, I lived the life of an independent working woman, cooking my own dinners, playing the big girl, before my mam and I made up and I returned home.

My boyfriend didn't share any of my budding dreams about making something of my life, and I was working so much we barely had time to see each other. With my new-found confidence, I decided we should break up.

At first, he seemed to take the news quite well. But after a week or two, he showed up one night outside work as I finished for the evening. He was there again the next night and the night after that. He asked me about the men I worked with, who they were, why I was laughing with them, which one of them I fancied. He began hanging around the alleyway I had to pass through on my way home.

Each time I met him he asked me to get back with him. He told me he loved me and how things would be different this time. He knew everything about my life and how much I craved stability. It really didn't take too much persuading to get me to change my mind. Soon, we were back together.

I quit my job and went back to Youthreach. I was getting paid to go to school, so I still had a little bit of my own money. I got incredible support from the teachers in that project. I discovered I loved learning just as much as ever, and I enjoyed engaging with the teachers and asking questions.

In late 2006, through Youthreach, I was chosen to take part in a consultation process with teenagers around the country about the age of consent for sexual activity. This was a project set up by the government after a court ruling earlier in the year. Two hundred and ten young people around the country were consulted, including me. I was passionate about the subject, for a very good reason! My boyfriend was two years older than I was, and I didn't think it was fair that he could be charged with statutory rape when we were in a consensual relationship.

I spoke so well at the consultation that I was invited back in November that year to meet the Minister for Children, Brian Lenihan, in his office to discuss the matter further. I could hardly believe it when I received the invitation from the minister's office in the post. Just seven of us were asked to come to Dublin to represent the views of all the participants. I was selected to talk about the issues on television, and my photograph appeared in the newspapers again. This time I was in Leinster House, discussing legislation and policy with a government minister. I'd come a long way since being pictured as a sulky frog!

My views on the age of consent were published in the *Irish Times*. I apparently said that 'people are growing up fast these days' – which was certainly true in my case! – and that 'teenagers will do it when they're ready to do it'. The minister was really friendly to us and I felt really special, for once, to have been picked to take part.

My report sheets from Youthreach were glowing. Teachers described me as an 'excellent student' and 'a pleasure to teach'. But my attendance was still poor. Sometimes I just didn't want to go, or there was so much chaos in my life that school wasn't a priority. My boyfriend didn't encourage me to keep going. He was very possessive, and I would feel guilty if I talked to other boys or even to male teachers. Having left school at a very young age himself, he didn't place any value on education.

When I first suggested to him that we should have a baby together, I think I was trying to wind him up. In a way, I wanted to find a way to get him to break up with me permanently, hoping he'd lose interest in me if I suggested having a child. At the same time, my mind was pretty confused. I had been thinking about getting pregnant for quite a while, for all the wrong reasons. I wanted my own home, my own little bubble of safety and love. I thought that was what having a baby would mean, even if I wasn't really one hundred per cent sure I wanted to have a baby with him.

What shocked me about my boyfriend's response was that he didn't immediately say no. He hesitated and said 'maybe'. Suddenly, it became a real possibility. Looking back on it, it seems so stupid and so naïve of me, but I was totally flattered. I felt privileged that someone – anyone! – would want to have that kind of lasting connection with me. This bad boy wanted to have a baby with me! Or at least he hadn't said no.

We went on as before, although we weren't taking any precautions to avoid pregnancy. We didn't talk about it much when we were together, but I dreamed every night about what a baby could mean for my life. I was determined not to repeat what my parents had done. To me, having a child meant staying with someone for ever. It would mean I'd finally have that happy family I'd hoped for – a mammy, a daddy and a baby. I'd have my own little unit – everything was going to be all right.

3

PREGNANT

Groggy and nauseous, I opened my eyes and immediately squeezed them shut again against the bright light shining above me. All I could hear was a loud, intermittent beeping sound. Where was I?

'Amy?' A woman's voice called my name. 'Amy? Are you awake?' I opened my eyes again, but the most I could manage in response to the woman was a grunt. Slowly, I took in my surroundings. I was lying in a bed, wrapped in what seemed to be some kind of foil blanket. The beeping was coming from a machine near my head. The woman, who was still hovering beside me, was in a nurse's uniform, and I became aware of others in the room. My boyfriend was sitting beside me, white as a sheet, with tears in his eyes. I could see his mother and his mother's friend. They also seemed to be crying.

I shut my eyes once more. Now, unfortunately, I remembered

everything. It was the end of January 2007. I was back living with my mam, but things had not been going well. I was also now firmly back together with my boyfriend, and we spent most of our time roaming the streets of Drogheda or hanging out in the fields above the town.

Mam's life had gone a bit further off the rails too. People I'd never met before were drinking in the house with her. When she went out, she would often go missing for hours. I craved some kind of 'normal' life, and I know my mam was trying to deal with her issues. During those years, she was constantly trying to sort herself out. But at that point we were both grappling with our problems in our own self-destructive ways, and we didn't seem to be able to stop.

We were rowing a lot – really ugly, nasty rows, sometimes on the verge of getting physical. There had been one on this particular evening. Mam said she had to go out, and I didn't want her to go. If she went out, I knew there was no way she would return sober, if she came back at all. She wouldn't hear of staying home, though. She was involved in a drama group with some people she had met at the local community centre. She was in a play that night, she said, and she couldn't let the others down. I didn't care what she was doing. I just wanted her to stay.

At that time, we were living in a small, terraced house on Bredin Street in Drogheda. The front door led straight out onto the street from our living room. Mam was standing with one hand on the door. She had her coat on and her bag over her shoulder. I was further back, standing beside the kitchen table. Mam had left her tablets there. I didn't even know what they were at the time, although afterwards I was told they were Xanax and Lexapro – anti-anxiety and anti-depression medication. In my mind, the tablets were part of the problem. Mam had been prescribed them and was still drinking. I didn't think she was ever really with it.

I grabbed the tubs and poured myself a handful of each. 'I'm going to take these!' I shouted at her, showing her the tablets in my fist. 'If you go, I'll swallow them!' Mam looked at me sceptically. She was well used to my dramatic gestures and did not for one moment expect me to follow through on my threat. She walked out and closed the door behind her. I put the tablets in my mouth and, before I knew it, I had swallowed them. I don't know what got into me – it could have simply been a reflex action. All I know is that I certainly didn't intend to kill myself. I was completely aware that I was looking for attention. I got a lot more of it than I had bargained for.

I started to panic immediately. I grabbed my phone and tried to call Mam. But it was like one of those bad dreams – in my panic I kept hitting the wrong buttons, and when I eventually managed to call the right number, her phone went straight to voicemail. I was now feeling faint, but I remembered there was an out-of-hours doctor on call at the Drogheda Cottage Hospital, around 500 metres away. I ran out of the house and collapsed in the doorway of the surgery, where they called an ambulance. The last thing I remembered before passing out was asking one of the nurses if I was going to die. I was terrified and realised that no one knew where I was. The nurse didn't give me much reassurance. She looked at me for a second before replying, 'I don't know.'

In the hospital room, as I remembered these details, I slowly started to come to. My boyfriend was still looking at me as if he was staring at death itself. I was definitely not a pretty sight, wrapped up in blankets, attached to tubes, my skin a greeny-grey colour. I felt like hell, but I was thankful to be alive.

I had been awake for just a couple of minutes when the door of the room flew open and Mam arrived in. Like everyone else, she was extremely distressed and ran to me, crying and hugging me. I was glad to see her, but I didn't have much sympathy for her: she hadn't been there when I needed her. The nurse spoke again. She told my mam that I was lucky to have made it through, that my blood pressure and all my vital signs had gone crazy. When the nurse left, my mam held my hand and asked me what I was thinking and why I'd done it. I didn't have an answer, and no one in the room really expected one. We all knew how chaotic my life had been for a long time.

Mam was devastated by what had happened. She was also deeply angry and upset with me that I had done such a stupid thing and that I had come so close to losing my life. I went back home, but not long afterwards we had another row. This time, the tension between us finally became physical and she hit me. I find it difficult to remember exactly what happened. It was the lowest point of our relationship, and I think I've made myself blank out many of the details. I told my solicitor a couple of months later that I had called an ambulance for myself, but I no longer remember doing that. All I know is that I ended up back in the emergency department of Our Lady of Lourdes Hospital.

There was no more talk about going into care voluntarily. It was clear our relationship was broken and living together was unsustainable. The social workers stepped in and this time they went to court. I was made the subject of an emergency care order by the district court, followed by an interim care order, putting me in the temporary care of the Health Service Executive. My mam promised that now she really would get the help she needed.

I hoped with all my heart that this time would be different and that Mam would manage to sort herself out once and for all. The truth was that, just as our relationship was at its worst, I was going to need her more than ever. My admission to hospital had confirmed what I had begun to suspect: I was pregnant.

I was still a bit overwhelmed by everything that had happened when a midwife came into the hospital room carrying what looked like a little walkie-talkie with a microphone attached. She smiled reassuringly at me. 'Will we check on the baby?' she asked. She felt my stomach gently, and then asked me if I would like to hear the baby's heartbeat. I nodded and she told me not to worry if we didn't hear anything. 'Sometimes we have to wait until you're a bit further along,' she said.

She explained that the gadget she was carrying was actually a foetal Doppler. 'This will feel cold,' she said as she squeezed some gel onto my still flat stomach. She placed the Doppler's wand on my tummy. I held my breath but there was no sound. 'Don't worry!' she said as she moved the wand all around, trying to find what she was looking for. Suddenly there was a crackle from the speaker, and the unmistakable sound of a heartbeat filled the room. 'It's a bit faster than yours,' the midwife said. I began crying, with relief and joy. I was sure the life I was bringing into this world would change my own life. Nothing mattered to me except the perfect little family I would soon have.

Our own families quickly adjusted to the news. Even

though we were so young, they accepted the pregnancy fully. In fact, they were delighted. There was no question about whether or not we would keep the baby. It wasn't something that was up for discussion. My views at the time were very black and white. To me, abortion was murder. There was no way I would have considered it and, in any case, I badly wanted this child, as did everyone else.

I was suddenly surrounded by the kind of love and support I had craved for so many years. I didn't think my boyfriend's mother liked me very much, but she had a new attitude towards me now I was carrying her grandchild. She often cooked big roast dinners for her sons. Now I was around the table as well, and she fed me turnip and broccoli and mashed potatoes to beat the band. She joined the baby clubs in her local pharmacy, and a corner of her living room was set aside for multiple packs of baby wipes and nappies. This would be the first grandchild on either side of the family and she could hardly wait.

Although our relationship was extremely strained, my mam was happy for us too. But she was also worried about me and my future. Sharon was born when Mam was only 19, and she knew how hard it was going to be for me.

Once again, however, the safe, steady family environment she had imagined for me when she couldn't care for me herself didn't materialise. I found myself in bed-and-breakfast accommodation in a huge house in the village of Slane, around

20 minutes' drive from Drogheda. The B&B was used by everyone – ordinary tourists, people working in the local area and children who were in trouble and in care, just like me.

Because I was pregnant, my boyfriend was allowed to stay with me in my room. His own house was so full of people that he didn't have a bed and he slept on the couch, which was where I had to sleep too when I stayed there. I loved when he stayed with me instead. I had sold my moped and had no easy way of travelling back into Drogheda from Slane. I didn't have any family around me and was completely dependent on him – without him, I felt I had no one. He knew this, of course, and it wasn't a healthy way to continue our relationship, but for a while we were happy.

When he stayed, we would chat about names for the baby and what our lives would be like. We dreamed of getting a house once the baby came and doing up a nursery. Maybe we'd even get a puppy as well? We were like two children, playing house with Ken and Barbie dolls. It was a lovely bubble to live in for a while.

It was also the perfect reason to get involved in one of my favourite hobbies – shopping. We went to the baby shop on Stockwell Street in Drogheda and looked at all the fancy travel systems. We chose a unisex design – a grey and cream swirly pattern with a pram, car seat, buggy and even a matching bag. My boyfriend couldn't believe how much it cost, but we put a deposit on it there and then. Every week I popped to Mothercare or to Dunnes to pick up more bits and pieces. I bought a steriliser, bottles, nappies, vests, tiny hats and socks in neutral colours and, of course, lots and lots of cute little babygros. Naturally, I was determined my child was going to be the best dressed baby in town! I was nearly four months pregnant and I already had everything I needed to welcome my baby to the world.

My birthday on 23 April 2007 looked like it was going to be extra special. Not only was I turning 17, but I was 16 weeks pregnant and I was due to have my first big scan at the hospital. I was really excited, as I was hoping to get the best birthday present ever. We were expecting to find out the sex of the baby.

I had stayed in my boyfriend's house the previous night, and everyone was in celebratory mood in the morning. His mother showed me yet another hamper she had bought for the baby, full of clothes and nappies. She put on a big fry for everyone, and we chatted happily about the day to come over mugs of tea. 'What do you think,' my boyfriend asked, 'boy or girl?' I didn't know and I really didn't care – if the baby was healthy, I would be happy. I was young and strong, and it never crossed my mind that there could be any problems at all. I was looking forward so much to getting my first glimpse of our child.

The appointment was at nine thirty that morning. My boyfriend's mother waved us off as we got into the taxi and headed to the hospital. He made a big fuss of me all the way there and guided me through the doors as if I was a fragile and delicate jewel. 'I could get used to this kind of treatment,' I thought. It was the same hospital I'd been brought to twice in previous months. This, however, was a much happier occasion. As we waited to be called for our scan, my boyfriend and I were giggling away, like little children ourselves.

The nurse who called us in didn't seem that much older than us. She was kind and friendly and we chatted for a while about pregnancy. She gave me lots of advice about what I should and shouldn't be eating and drinking. She asked me if I was taking care of myself, and she explained what I could expect over the months to come. Finally, she dimmed the lights and directed me up on the couch, pointing out the screen where I would see my baby for the first time. She told me to lie down and lift up my top while she squirted the ultrasound gel all over my tiny bump. I jumped and squealed at how cold it was and we all started laughing. Then she got her probe and began rubbing it on my belly.

A black-and-white image popped up on the screen, and I

gestured excitedly to my boyfriend. We could see the baby's legs moving, then its hands opening and closing. The room filled with the sound of its heart, still beating away loudly and quickly. The nurse pointed out parts of the baby's body to me. She asked us if we wanted to know whether it was a girl or boy. We nodded enthusiastically, and she told us she thought the baby was a girl. My boyfriend couldn't stop grinning.

We both continued staring intently at the screen, but it was hard to tell what we were looking at. I turned towards the midwife to ask her a question, and that's when I noticed she had stopped smiling. She was pressing buttons on her keypad and zooming in on a particular part of the image. Her brow was furrowed and she seemed very confused. 'Just a second,' she said, 'I need to get the doctor in here to check something.'

My boyfriend and I looked at each other, afraid to say a word. The image on the screen wasn't very clear, and I couldn't tell what had caused the nurse such obvious concern. I tried to fight the sick feeling that was growing in my stomach.

Within minutes, she was back in the room, this time with an older man who introduced himself as a consultant doctor. Now we were all staring at the screen as they adjusted the image and murmured quietly to each other. I was beginning to panic, and all my worst fears were confirmed when the consultant turned to me: 'I'm sorry, Miss Dunne,' he said, 'we can't see the baby's head.'

Time seemed to stop for a moment. I had no idea what he was talking about. What did he mean he couldn't see the head? Surely there must be something wrong with their machine? Or maybe the baby was just hiding from the probe? He continued talking and I forced myself to try to listen to what he was saying. He told us our baby had a condition that meant her head had not developed properly. She had no skull and would not survive outside my womb. She was going to die.

I needed to vomit. I pulled down my shirt and jumped off the bed, even as the doctor was continuing to talk. Crying and screaming, I ran out of the hospital, not caring who could hear me, my boyfriend running behind me, calling my name. Outside, he managed to calm me down a little and persuaded me to get into a taxi where I rang my mam, sobbing hysterically as I tried to speak. 'Mam … Mam … the baby … there's no head, Mam … it has no head …'

She didn't know what was going on. 'Take a deep breath, Amy, it'll be OK.' She asked to speak to my boyfriend. 'Mind her,' she told him, and she arranged to meet us back at his house.

His family were already gathered, eagerly waiting to hear the result of our scan. I ran in and told them all that it wasn't happening. There would be no little baby, no first grandchild. The baby was broken and we didn't know what to do. My mother arrived and both of our mothers tried to calm me down. No one could understand what I was saying. I couldn't even remember the name of the condition the consultant had mentioned. My mam thought I must be overreacting, as usual. Both mothers decided they would go back to the hospital themselves and told me to relax until we found out more.

While they were gone, I began freaking out. I lay on the couch, bawling crying, wanting to throw up. I felt as if there was an alien in my belly. Part of me still hoped that Mam would come back from the hospital and tell me I'd got it wrong. But in my heart, I knew that wasn't going to happen. I had seen the faces of the nurse and doctor as they looked at the scan. This wasn't a normal healthy baby. I looked down at my stomach – I wanted to turn my skin inside out and get this thing out of me. We'd found out we were going to have a girl, but she was never going to be my little girl.

Our mothers returned, both of them with tears in their eyes. Mam put her arms around me and held me tight. They had managed to speak to the doctor, and he had told them I was not exaggerating the seriousness of my baby's condition. She was unlikely to survive even one day after the birth. They had the official report of the scan. It stated that a 'foetal abnormality was noted'. The nurse had been unable to get the usual measurement of the baby's skull. Brain tissue could be seen and no 'cranial vault was noted'. They had written down the name of the condition the doctor had diagnosed – anencephaly.

No one knew what to do. None of us had ever heard of this condition or anything like it. I immediately wanted to know more. My boyfriend's family had a computer in the sitting room, and I did the worst thing anyone could possibly do in such a situation – I opened up Google.

I must have sat there for hours, staring at photographs of all these little babies with this deadly deformity, polluting my mind. The pictures of the children were very disturbing. Tears running down my face, I scrolled through image after horrifying image of babies with no skulls. There were images of scans, more detailed pictures from inside the womb, photographs of the babies after they had been born. I watched videos; I studied survival rates and tried to figure it out. Surely, I thought, there had to be some way around this.

I searched for words of optimism or reassurance, for stories about miracles, but there were none. These babies never survived. They might take a breath of air and, in rare cases, live for a few days, but it was serious and always fatal. The choice for a mother in this situation, it seemed, was to end the pregnancy immediately or make the decision to carry the baby to full term, knowing he or she might not survive the birth and would certainly die soon afterwards. There were no other options. I put my hand on my belly and knew my daughter had no chance.

The more I read, the more I blamed myself. Folic acid was supposed to prevent these kinds of conditions. I hadn't taken folic acid regularly, even though I'd wanted to get pregnant. This was, I believed, all my fault.

All around me, people were going on with their normal lives, making tea, going shopping, playing outside. A friend of my boyfriend's popped in to wish me a happy birthday but left again pretty quickly. Everyone was detached from this issue while I had the issue attached to my body. I wanted the situation to end as quickly as possible, but I didn't know how to make that happen.

Tentatively, I typed the word 'abortion' into the search engine. It just made me feel worse. I read about the different types of procedures you could have and exactly what was involved in each one. Plenty of images and videos accompanied the explanations, and I was grossed out. Some of the videos were, of course, deliberately meant to disgust and upset anyone contemplating an abortion. They worked.

I already absolutely hated the thought of abortion, even before watching the videos. If I had considered it at all during my 17 years, I had thought of it as the murder of an innocent baby. I thought it was disgusting for people to have abortions when there were so many people who wanted children and couldn't have them. If you don't want a baby, make sure you don't get pregnant was how I saw it. I said all the kinds of things that are easy to say when you're not in the situation I was now in.

My mind was exhausted and my head ached. My bloated belly repulsed me, and I snapped at anyone who tried to talk to me. I didn't think of this thing inside me as a baby and I wanted it gone. No one could understand what I was going through. When I eventually managed to close my eyes that night, I had terrible nightmares, full of the images I had been looking at. As soon as I woke the following morning, the horror hit me all over again.

Mam called over to see me and persuaded me out for a walk. We were able to talk honestly, with no one else around. Mam was broken-hearted for me. She had had a miscarriage herself, and she told me she understood what it was like to be pregnant and end up without a baby. She was also concerned that my boyfriend and I were both very young to be trying to deal with a tragedy like this.

She asked me to look at the situation and examine the pros and cons of each option – continuing with the pregnancy or having a termination immediately. As we talked, my mind began to clear a little. I had read on the internet about women in my situation who continued to carry their babies, but I knew this was something I personally couldn't contemplate.

Although I had wanted this baby so much, I couldn't imagine having to continue with the pregnancy for at least another five months. I felt sick to think of my belly growing even bigger and strangers asking me when I was due. I still felt as if there was a foreign body inside me and I wanted it removed.

My mam put her arm around me and told me she completely supported me, whatever I chose to do. 'I trust you to make the right decision for yourself, love,' she told me. When we went back to tell my boyfriend's mother, she felt the same. 'It's your choice, Amy,' she said. I was still distressed and traumatised, but I began to feel slightly relieved. At least the choice had been made.

Of course, the next problem I faced was that this was not something I could do at home, although I was a bit hazy about exactly why not.

I knew that unborn children were protected in Ireland. Later, it was explained to me that this was because of a referendum in 1983, when a majority of Irish people voted to put special wording into the constitution. This wording ensured that the right to life of 'the unborn' was protected equally with the mother's life. Then in 1992, when I was two years old, the country had been stunned by the case of a 14-year-old girl who became pregnant after being raped and wanted to travel to England to have an abortion. Her case became known as the 'X case', to protect her identity. Evidence was heard that the girl had been talking about ending her life and eventually the Supreme Court ruled she could travel. It decided that abortions were allowed where there was a real risk to the life of the mother, including the risk of suicide.

I had absolutely no clue how relevant all of this was about to become to my own life. I'm not even sure I was fully aware that abortion, in most cases, was actually against the law in Ireland. I thought that maybe it was just a procedure that wasn't done in Irish hospitals because the Catholic Church was against it. I personally still felt it was something shameful and wrong. But in the situation I was now in, I had come to the conclusion that it was the only option available to me – or at least the only option I could live with. One of the few certainties in my mind was that my child was going to die, and I needed to bring the situation to an end. I thought it was so obvious that I needed to do this that no one would even contemplate stopping me.

A further problem for me was my own personal situation. My mam fully supported what I wanted to do, but at that time, she wasn't the only adult who had authority over me. I was the subject of a care order, and there were social workers who were responsible for my wellbeing. I felt it was my duty to tell them what I was planning to do.

I've often wondered why I made the decision to tell them and what would have happened if I had just sneaked off to

England. Perhaps I was looking for help. I thought they might be able to guide me towards the right place to go. I probably also thought they might offer me some financial help. Maybe it was simply that, at heart, I was a good girl who liked to do things properly. They were supposed to be looking after me, and I needed to leave the country for a few days – I thought it was only right to let them know that I wouldn't be around. It was a decision that would change how the rest of my life would turn out.

The next morning, I headed up to the local health centre. It was, and still is, a pretty grim-looking place. It's in the middle of a field, without even a tree or a flower planted near it, a dark red-brick square box, with small windows set high up in the walls, cordoned off on one side by steel security fencing. I was looking for the social worker I usually dealt with, but she wasn't there, so they suggested I speak to her boss – the guy who was in charge of the team.

He brought me into a room that looked like an interview room in a police station. There was a table with two chairs on either side of it. The only natural light came from the small high windows. I told the social worker about my decision to travel to the UK. I explained to him that my boyfriend, his mother and my own mother were all supporting me and trying to raise money so we could make the trip.

I was distraught and I thought I'd get help. Instead, I felt he talked down to me and dismissed my feelings. He told me I had absolutely no choice about carrying this baby. Abortion was illegal in Ireland. Under the law, if I chose to abort this baby, he said, there was a risk I could be prosecuted. He explained that it was a very complicated legal situation and he would speak to the HSE's solicitor about it and come back to me. I couldn't believe what I was hearing, but I thought it was some kind of mistake that would be easily cleared up after he spoke to the solicitor.

I was wrong. That evening the same social worker rang me and said he'd spoken to the lawyers. I understood from what he said that they had already gone to court to stop me getting a termination, although it turned out that this was not the case. On a further call, he told me the HSE had taken action to stop me leaving the country. My passport had expired, and he told me I needed the HSE's consent to get a new one, as I was in its care. I was young and naïve and believed what I was being told by the people who had authority over me.

I told my mother what the social worker had said. As far as I was concerned, I was now trapped and there was no way out. I was going to have to continue the pregnancy and have the baby. The thoughts in my head were starting to scare me as I tried to think of ways to end the nightmare I was trapped in. How much alcohol would I have to drink? Could I throw myself down the stairs? Would a boiling-hot bath work? What could I do to help myself, now no one was going to help me?

Mam met with the same social worker, who told both her and my boyfriend's mother the same things. The HSE was acting as my parent. I wasn't allowed to leave the state without permission from the courts, and if we went without that permission, anyone who helped me or accompanied me would be an accessory to murder. My mother also told me she had been approached outside the health centre by someone who knew what was going on. This person gave my mother very simple advice for us both: 'get a solicitor'.

The next day, 26 April, I rang a solicitor's office in Dundalk and made an appointment to see him later that afternoon. My main concern at that point was how I was going to get a passport if the HSE wouldn't consent to my leaving the country. I hoped the solicitor would be able to help me with that. Shortly afterwards, however, I got a phone call from the social worker, who asked me to come up to the health centre to see him.

He told me that an appointment had been made for me to see a psychiatrist in Navan that afternoon. When I complained that would mean I wouldn't be able to get to my meeting with the solicitor, he told me that I would have to go to the psychiatric assessment, as it was urgent. He said he was concerned about me because I had told him I could not live through the pregnancy knowing my baby would die.

I didn't think he could possibly have believed that I meant I was going to kill myself. He was taking my words out of context. Of course I was distressed and upset, and I certainly said it would kill me to go through with the pregnancy, but I had no intention of harming myself. I was just trying to express my desperation at the situation I was in. Nevertheless, I felt I had no alternative but to give in and agree to go to the assessment.

I was brought by taxi to Our Lady's Hospital in Navan that afternoon, along with my boyfriend. It's funny the events that stay with you and affect you most in the years afterwards. It's not always the obvious things. The scenes I saw in hospital left some of the deepest scars.

The psychiatric unit in Navan was, to my teenage eyes, like something out of a horror movie. Everywhere was painted white. Along the corridors, patients who were much older than me sat staring out into the garden. One old man sat on a bench, staring glassy-eyed into space. He was so drugged, or just out of it, that he didn't even look up as we passed by. It traumatised me to see so many sad and broken people, and it still upsets me to think about them. I was terrified that I was going to end up in there with them.

I spoke to a psychiatrist for around 45 minutes, with my social worker in the room with us. He later claimed I had said I had no objection to him staying for the consultation. I don't remember being given that choice. Strangely, one of my most vivid memories from that consultation is being asked to count in sevens. The psychiatrist may have been trying to work out how well my brain was working and what kind of capacity I had to make decisions.

Afterwards, the social worker and the psychiatrist spoke to each other privately. They told me I was being excluded from their conversation because of my age, but I managed to overhear snippets from outside the door. I heard the social worker suggesting that the psychiatrist might have to appear in court.

The psychiatrist stated clearly in his assessment of me that I was not suicidal. He said I was completely sane and capable of making rational decisions, although he said I was suffering from stress due to the news about my baby's condition. It was, after all, still only three days since my 17th birthday and since I had been for my scan. After speaking to another colleague, he offered me a bed in the hospital for a few days' observation. I refused point blank to accept this. I needed this situation resolved *now*. There was no way I was going to spend the next few days lying in a bed in this terrifying place, looking at my belly and getting even more upset.

The social worker suggested to me that, even though I was not suicidal, I wasn't coping well and maybe I just needed a break. I remember him whispering into my ear that I should take the chance to stay a little while – 'take some medication, get some rest'. He later strongly denied that he had made this suggestion, but my memory of it is clear.

For once, my boyfriend's tendency to be possessive came in useful. He was annoyed at any suggestion that I would stay at the hospital instead of coming home and began to get angry with the social worker. We cleared off out of the place, his strong emotion giving me added strength to stick to my decision.

Something in me knew that if I gave in and stayed in the hospital, I would have little chance of getting to England. Of course, the HSE wanted the whole awkward situation to end. If I stayed in the hospital, maybe I'd change my mind. If I were found to be suicidal, an abortion would be deemed legal under Irish law and the situation would be much easier to manage. But I was not suicidal. And I was not like the poor broken people I had seen in the hospital. I was not going to be portrayed that way, and I wanted to fight with whatever strength I had left in me. I have always felt that if I don't get somewhere by telling the truth, then I am not meant to get there. Looking back, I don't know how I found the strength, but I was absolutely determined not to lie.

It was late that evening by the time we eventually got to my solicitor's offices. While I had been in the psychiatric hospital, the solicitor, Conor MacGuill, had been exchanging emails with the HSE's lawyers that afternoon. The correspondence that afternoon repeated what the social worker had told me – they would not consent to me going abroad to terminate my pregnancy, and they would not help.

The HSE's solicitor told my lawyer that the social worker had notified a local garda superintendent to get help from the Gardaí to stop me from leaving the country without a court order or the HSE's consent. The letter added, however, that the HSE would be willing to ask the district court for an order allowing me to go to the UK if it was shown that I was suicidal. If I had not agreed to go to the psychiatric assessment that afternoon, they had planned to get a court order to make me go. But because the assessment had shown no risk of suicide, it appeared they were simply going to expect me to continue with my pregnancy.

I was shocked to see it confirmed in writing. The social worker and the HSE were completely ignoring my wishes. They seemed to have no concern about what I was going through and had no appreciation for what I wanted or what might be in my best interests. It seemed clear that they weren't going to consent to me getting a passport, and if I tried to leave the country, I believed I was going to be arrested. All I wanted was to be able to manage my own personal trauma in as dignified and private a way as possible. The idea that I should just continue with the pregnancy seemed inhumane. I couldn't see how this would be in my interests.

During my consultation with my solicitor I started to realise that I had rights. I deserved to be able to do what I wanted with my body and to make the best decision for my child and for me. The solid childhood I'd had as a very young girl meant I knew right from wrong, and surely this was wrong. Now that I had a lawyer, I had a small bit of hope that I might have some power to do something about my situation.

It had become clear, however, that the only way we were going to be able to sort this out was to fight the HSE in court. It was late on a Thursday evening when I finished my consultation. As this was not a matter that could wait around too long, my solicitor began making arrangements for our case to be heard as soon as possible.

Just as we were heading to court, my mother had one last meeting with the social worker. He warned her that the case was going to become a 'media circus'. Mam was scared. She asked him if all the details about our relationship would be made public in the courtroom. 'You wouldn't know,' he replied.

4

COURT

kept my head down as my lawyers had told me to do. I concentrated on my mam's feet briskly tip-tapping just in front of me and gripped my boyfriend's hand hard in mine. As we got closer to the gates leading into the Four Courts building, the noise started to build and the shouting grew louder. I could only make out the odd word. 'Choice' was one; 'murderer' was another.

It was the fourth day of my case, just over a week since the scan that had changed everything. Everyone had told me to ignore the people outside, but I couldn't help sneaking a glance at the crowds lining the quays alongside the River Liffey. There seemed to be two groups, one on either side of the entrance to the courts. The larger group was spread out along the front of the imposing granite columns. Some had placards showing photographs of foetuses or aborted babies.

I recognised the images from the hours of endless googling I had been doing since my scan. They were being carried mainly by men and women old enough to be my grandparents, but there were also some younger people, and even a few children, among them. I kept staring, unable to look away. Slogans were written on some of the placards: 'She's a child, not a choice', 'Abortion is for ever', and one that almost made me lose the composure I was trying so hard to cling on to: 'Pro-choice = a death sentence for the disabled'.

My whole body began to shake. The old man in the brown tweed suit and grey cloth cap holding this particular placard wasn't even looking at me. He was staring at the ground, muttering, almost in a trance, as he waved the poster someone had clearly gone to some trouble to make. I wanted to scream and shout, rant and rave. I wanted to rip his stupid placard out of his hands and fling it into the busy traffic. How dare a man stand there, a man who had never carried a child, and accuse me of wanting to kill disabled children? These people didn't even understand my daughter's condition.

The smaller group on the other side of the entrance was made up of people supporting me and my right to choose what to do. But with the noise and the stress, it was hard for me to work out exactly who was who. I put my head down again and lowered my eyes. I didn't want any of these people to see into my soul. I followed my mam and my solicitor quickly through the gates and into the relative calm of the courtyard, thankful I had survived that part of my daily ordeal without losing my cool for one more morning.

We had ended up in the High Court, taking on the organisation responsible for running the health service, within four days of my consultation with a lawyer. Conor, the solicitor, had asked me lots of questions and had written down all my answers in a document that I then I had to sign. I felt a bit worried and uneasy, as I had to tell him about my relationship with my mother and about the events that had led to me discovering I was pregnant and being taken into care. I didn't really want to tell him all about my life, and I knew my mother would be devastated that these parts of our lives were being discussed. I tried to say as little as possible, but some details could not be avoided. He assured me that he would turn it all into a proper legal document.

It was out of my control now. I had no choice but to stay on this rollercoaster and see where we would end up. I focused on putting on a brave face for the court. As usual, I tried to look my best and dress as appropriately as I could for the situation. On the evening before our very first day in court, I laid out my outfit for our trip to Dublin. I chose a white maternity dress with black daisies printed on it, some leggings and little black shoes. I was living between the B&B and my boyfriend's house and I didn't have a lot, but of course, I didn't want that to be obvious to the world. I wanted to show people I was not broken.

Over the previous five years, I'd seen my mam fall apart. I knew you could tell so much about someone from the way they were dressed and the way they held themselves. I was a person who understood love and self-respect, I hadn't fallen to pieces, and I wanted people to know that. As the court case began, I was still in my little bubble. I was still Amy Dunne, and this was still my private problem. My pain wasn't yet on view for the entire country to analyse.

My boyfriend and I arrived early in a taxi from Drogheda on that first day, not really knowing where we were going. We'd seen pictures of the big grey building on the television before, but we didn't even know what a 'high court' was. My solicitor had an office nearby, where he met us before escorting us into the main courts complex. I was petrified that everyone would immediately know who we were and what we were doing. But we walked into the building, unnoticed, among the crowds of lawyers, gardaí, prison officers, handcuffed criminals and ordinary members of the public.

What we noticed first was the buzz of conversation. In the echoey round hall, at the centre of the building, every space was filled by huddles of people, all talking loudly at each other. We looked around, confused, until Conor directed us up a long, twisting staircase that seemed to go on for ever.

We went right up to the top, until we reached courtroom number 16.

The corridors were full of barristers rushing in all directions, their long black robes flowing behind them. Some wore strange-looking wigs. I had only ever seen people dressed like that on television shows. Everyone seemed so much older than us.

In the corridor outside the courtroom, Conor introduced me to my own barristers. There were two men and a woman – an older man as well as a younger man and an even younger woman. 'This is Mr Fitzsimons, Mr Hogan and Ms Phelan,' he said. 'You are in the very best of hands.' I didn't know it at the time, but I had some of the best constitutional lawyers in the country acting on my behalf. All I cared about was that they would have my best interests at heart.

The legal team introduced themselves and shook our hands. The older man had white hair and twinkly eyes behind his glasses. The woman was kind and friendly. They all tried to prepare me for what was going to happen, but it was so completely alien to me that it was hard to take in much of what they were saying. They explained that the first step we had to take was to get permission from the High Court judge to take our challenge against the Health Service Executive. I wasn't sure exactly what was going on. I wasn't entirely sure what we were hoping to achieve in the court. I just wanted to get a passport and go. My boyfriend looked equally stunned and confused by it all. He had gone from being a wild teenager, running around the streets of Drogheda, to being completely out of his depth in this totally bizarre environment.

The courtroom was packed, and we had to push through the crowd gathered at the door to get in. It wasn't my idea of what a court should look like or what I'd seen on television. It was a fairly drab, normal-looking space, with a shabby carpet and peeling light-blue paint on the walls. The only indication that it was more than an ordinary meeting room was the harp in the centre of the wall at the top of the room, over a bench that was higher than all the others. My solicitor directed us to sit in the few remaining spaces on the wooden benches facing the harp. Every seat filled up, and men and women in wigs and black robes were standing all around us, most of them clutching folders of papers. Conor headed up to sit with the other solicitors at the top of the room.

Suddenly, a man appeared out of another doorway, to the right of the harp, and everyone sitting on the benches jumped to their feet. The man looked to me like a mad professor, wearing a wig from under which wisps of curly, unruly hair peeked out and a pair of steel-rimmed glasses. He made his way to the bench, and when he sat down we all sat again too. This was Mr Justice William McKechnie, I was told later, the man who would decide my fate.

The woman sitting in front of the judge called out different names and numbers. As she did so, various lawyers popped up and spoke to the judge. It was all very fast and almost incomprehensible to me. I knew they had reached my case when my solicitor nodded his head towards me and I heard my boyfriend's name being called out. My own name wasn't mentioned – I was to be known as 'Miss D', as I was under 18 and entitled to anonymity. The case had to be taken on my behalf by an adult. My boyfriend was able to do this as he was two years older than me. He was to be known legally as my 'next friend'. We both found this hilarious, and I had to stop myself from laughing out loud despite how scared I was.

The younger male barrister on my team – Mr Hogan, who was small and dark-haired with kind eyes and a very posh voice – got to his feet and began explaining my predicament to the judge. I was four months pregnant, he said, with a baby who had a life expectancy of three days at most. He said I hadn't even considered abortion until I had learned of my baby's condition, but now I wanted to travel. He told the judge it was very urgent. He said I wanted the court to quash the HSE's decision not to allow me to travel unless I was suicidal. And, he said, I wanted the court to order the HSE to tell the Gardaí that they consented to me travelling to the UK.

The hearing didn't take too long. The judge said the HSE and the state should have their lawyers in court before things went any further, and he asked my legal team to consider if my mother should also be represented by lawyers. We were able to escape the packed, stuffy room after just a couple of minutes, although the lawyers explained that we'd have to come back the following day when everyone else would also get a chance to speak to the judge.

I looked at my boyfriend. That didn't seem so bad, I thought. In my head, it all seemed pretty straightforward. I thought we'd just come back the next day, explain again what had gone on, the judge would see how ridiculous the whole thing was, and it would all be over. I didn't understand the controversy and consternation my case would cause.

There was something else I hadn't realised: one of the people in court was not a barrister or a solicitor but a court reporter, whose job it was to take note of any interesting cases and report on them for the newspapers. A general election campaign was underway at the time. I was a 17-year-old girl whose case went to the heart of a political fight and religious battle that had been underway since well before I was born. Even though we had been in court for just a few minutes, I was about to become the centre of a major news story.

I woke up early the next morning and headed into the kitchen to get some breakfast. I was in my boyfriend's house, and his mother was already up making tea. From the way she looked at me, I knew something was wrong. 'Amy ...' she said, 'you're in the papers.' The blood drained from my face. How could this have happened? It turned out she had been out to the corner shop just beside the house and had seen my story all over the papers. My lawyers' ten-minute presentation in the court the previous day had made the front pages. The *Irish Independent* was leading with a story about 'fears of a legal crisis' – over me! The story was also on the front page of the *Irish Times*. I felt weak. How could this be anyone else's business? In my head, it wasn't even really my partner's business. This child was in me, and it seemed the simplest decision in the world to allow me to travel to England and deal with this terrible tragedy in the way I wanted to. Suddenly, the whole country was going to have a say.

I lost my appetite. I dressed quickly, and we called a taxi and headed for the courts. This time my mam and my boyfriend's mam came with us. My solicitor rang and said he would meet us again at his office and walk in with us. Protesters had already started to gather outside, although the groups were still small in number at this stage.

I was shocked to see cameramen with big television cameras as well as several photographers waiting outside the gate. 'Ignore them all,' Conor said. I did what I was told. I knew everyone at the gates must have known I was the girl being talked about inside. I was very petite, meaning my bump was already quite visible. Who else could I be except Miss D, the person I seemed to have transformed into overnight? My solicitor explained that the media couldn't publish any pictures of me or anyone associated with me, as the court had ordered that my identity was not to be revealed. But I was still distressed that the cameras were there.

The hearing was expected to take a lot longer than the previous day's proceedings. We were in a different courtroom this time. We went into a red-brick building, which looked like an office block, beside the main entrance and travelled up in a tiny, ancient lift to the top floor. I was already feeling sick, and the lift went so fast, it felt like my stomach was left behind on the ground. If yesterday's room had been slightly shabby and underwhelming, this one was even shabbier, as well as being dark and absolutely tiny. In fact, the courtroom was too small for all the people who wanted to be there, and crowds were already waiting outside in the corridor. I stood there with them, held my boyfriend's hand and looked at my mother's worried face. I had a bad feeling about all of it.

The judge still had a number of other matters to hear before he got to our case, so we had to wait outside. 'I need air,' my mam said, and she disappeared back towards the lifts. Minutes later, our solicitor popped his head out to call us in. I pushed in to the stuffy courtroom to see the barrister who had spoken on my behalf the previous day talking to the judge again. The first thing he said was that my mother was in the building, that she supported me and was willing to go along with whatever I decided. The judge may have looked like a crazy professor, but his eyes were kind and he spoke with care. He asked for someone to find my mother and ask her to come into the courtroom, and he said she should be represented by lawyers. 'Whatever differences there may have been in the past between mother and daughter,' the judge said, 'it would be unthinkable if she was not represented.' When Mam came into court, she explained to the judge that she could not afford lawyers and needed legal aid. Lawyers for the HSE said that if an application for legal aid couldn't be processed quickly enough, they would fund my mam's lawyers.

I left the courtroom myself at this point, as I thought I was going to faint from the heat and the sheer number of people packed into the tiny room. I pushed my way through the door and went outside to catch my breath. This meant I missed the rest of what my barrister told the judge. Afterwards, I was told that he read out, in full, the legal document I had prepared with my solicitor the previous week.

I know now, of course, that this is part of how court cases work. For me to get permission from the judge to take my case against the HSE, the lawyer had to explain my reasons. Reading out my sworn document or affidavit, as it's called, had to be done to show that our action was justified. Looking back, I'm sure the lawyers probably told me all of this in advance. But all I can remember is being horrified to find out that my personal details had been broadcast to all those strangers in that tiny, stuffy little courtroom.

The judge was told that my father didn't want any involvement with me, that I'd left school, that my mam was an alcoholic, that there'd been a row at home, that I lived in a bed and breakfast. My whole life was reduced to these bare facts. All my happy childhood years, all my effort to work and to put on a front counted for nothing. In court, I was just one more tragic, fatherless, disadvantaged girl in the care of the state, probably one of many the lawyers came across every day. I knew my mam would have been devastated to hear all this. I remember being relieved that she has always had severe difficulties with her hearing. During the entire case, she had real trouble hearing anything that anyone in court said.

My lawyer also described to the judge how distressed I was when I found out how serious my baby's condition was and that she would not survive outside my womb. And he told the court that social workers had tried to have me admitted to a psychiatric hospital.

Lawyers for the HSE told the court they wanted to do whatever was best for me, subject to the care order that was in force in my case. They also said they were anxious to have me psychiatrically assessed again. My lawyers emphasised to the judge that I was not suicidal. It was true that I had said to whoever would listen that carrying on with the pregnancy would kill me, but there was no way I really wanted to die. What I had done a few months before was a cry for help, a plea to my mother, nothing more. I wanted to make sure people knew that I was not mentally ill, that I was not addicted to drink or drugs, that I knew my own mind.

The proceedings were just coming to an end by the time I decided I could face going back into court. As I stood at the back with my mam, she tried to put her arm around me. I shook it off and sat down. I was annoyed with her and with everyone else in the courtroom. I felt all this arguing was a waste of valuable time. My stomach was growing every day. I just wanted this over and done with.

The judge said he was giving me permission to take my legal action. I looked around, trying to catch my lawyers' eyes. I was relieved and thought that was the end of it. I'd won; the case was over – wasn't it? To my disappointment, the judge went on to say we would all have to come back to court in a couple of days' time for the arguments to be fully heard. I didn't understand the process and I was extremely frustrated. I felt it was all going far too slowly. I didn't realise that, because of my growing bump, my case was actually being rushed through the courts at a speed unheard of in the legal system.

We returned to court two days later. By now, my story was headline news across the country, and the protesters from both sides were outside in large numbers. Miss D was on the front of every newspaper, on every radio station, on every television news bulletin. The social worker's ominous warning to my mam about a 'media circus' had turned out to be correct, and we were cracking under the strain.

My life at that time had become very strange. All my relationships had gone sour. The social workers who had been supporting me couldn't really be there for me because I was taking the organisation that employed them to court. My mam was still struggling with alcoholism, and my boyfriend, even though he was older than me, was still just a teenager himself. I thought I had done the right thing by going to the people who were supposed to be caring for me and asking for help, but I was being treated as if I had done something wrong.

Mam was making a big effort to support me. She knew how important it was to be there, but it was difficult for her. The newspapers had reported all the details I had described in my document for my solicitor. There was no room for nuance in the black-and-white news reports, no explanation of the difficulties and events that had led each of us to this point in our lives. Communication had broken down between us. We were barely speaking to each other, but she was determined to be with me.

The same couldn't be said for my boyfriend. He was doing his best to be supportive, but sitting in court for hours, listening to people talk, was boring and almost incomprehensible to him. I could understand how he felt – is there any teenager who would want to sit through legal jargon for four or five hours every day? That morning I'd had to beg him to come with us. He didn't see the point of sitting there and told me we'd find out what happened afterwards on the radio or television. I, on the other hand, wanted to know everything that was going on with my body and my baby. The atmosphere in the taxi on the way in with my mother, my boyfriend and me had been pretty tense.

It had been suggested to me that we didn't need to get a taxi every day, as there was a regular bus from Drogheda to Dublin. But I refused to get the bus – I was afraid people would know who I was, and I didn't even know how to get to the High Court from the bus station. My solicitor stepped in and ensured that we continued to get a taxi.

After making our way through the protesters outside, past the man in the brown tweed suit, we made our way to court for the full hearing. We were in a much larger courtroom this time, but it was already packed with people. My boyfriend and I looked around in confusion – there was nowhere for us to sit. Conor managed to persuade some bystanders to make space, and we squashed onto one of the benches, but every time we left the room, I was worried there would be nowhere for us to go when we came back. I was annoyed and stressed out – if this case was all about me, why didn't I even have a proper seat in the court? And anyway, who were all these people?

My solicitor explained that the courts were open for anyone who wanted to be there. I hadn't realised this. I thought the only people allowed to be there were the people connected with the case and the journalists. That, to me, was bad enough. But my lawyers told me court cases were supposed to be heard in public, and the public were entitled to attend. Anyone, from anywhere, was allowed to come and hear all about my private business. It made me more paranoid, as well as embarrassed and ashamed that my life was being talked about in such a public way.

Five sets of legal teams were now lined up in court, with some of the top lawyers in the country involved. Of the 12 main barristers, only four of them were women. There were separate teams representing me, my mother, the HSE, the state and, strangest of all for me, my baby or 'the unborn' as she was called, legally. I found out that lawyers for the state had gone into court the previous day to tell the judge the 'unborn' would be legally represented at the hearing, but I wasn't required to be in court when that was done. We were all in separate little legal bubbles. I found it strange that my mam was now a part of the case and had her own 'people'. I didn't understand that her case was supporting the arguments being made by my lawyers.

The proceedings got underway, and I tried to concentrate on what was being said. One of my other barristers was speaking this time – Mr Fitzsimons, the white-haired, tallest and oldest member of my team. He read out the report written by the psychiatrist I had been brought to on the day I was supposed to be visiting my solicitor. This psychiatrist had concluded I was not suicidal and had no psychiatric illness. 'Well, of course not,' I thought to myself angrily. Why were they wasting time telling the court what seemed to me to be obvious? Mr Fitzsimons said the HSE had told me I wasn't allowed to travel. The social worker had phoned a garda superintendent and followed up by writing to him asking gardaí to stop me if I tried to leave the country. Apparently, the superintendent had written back, saying the guards had no power to do such a thing and would not arrest me unless there was a court order directing them to do so. This was something we hadn't known a few days previously. The HSE, Mr Fitzsimons said, was making the case that it had done its duty but, he said, it had got the law very wrong.

He gave the judge a report from an obstetrician. This doctor said that continuing with the pregnancy posed a risk to me because of my young age and the desperate condition of the baby. Because the baby's prognosis was so hopeless and she was going to die within such a short time, Mr Fitzsimons argued the procedure I was going to have wouldn't be a termination 'in the traditional meaning'. It was possible it wouldn't count under abortion laws and could be done in Ireland. For a minute, I felt the first spark of hope I had felt since the morning of the scan. Was there a chance that I wouldn't need to have what I considered an 'abortion' and I might not even need to leave the country? I put my hand on my bump and hoped he was right.

Just then, the judge interrupted. 'I think you should read out the results of her scan in open court, Mr Fitzsimons,' he said. I squeezed my boyfriend's hand and looked at the lawyers in shock. I knew what it said, but I didn't want to hear it again. As my barrister began to read the consultant's report, detailing the fact that my baby did not have a skull or a 'cranial vault', as they put it, I felt hot and faint. Tears ran down my face. I couldn't listen to this, in front of all these people. I grabbed my boyfriend and ran for the door, just as I had in the hospital. My mam and my solicitor came out after me. Conor explained to me that it was important that the details were made public, so that everyone would know just how serious my situation was. The judge needed to have all the details fully explained to him in order to make his decision.

I knew he was right, but I wondered why no one seemed to

care how this would make me feel. No one asked my opinion. All I wanted was to have my sick baby taken out of my body. I didn't understand why so many people had to be so involved in my personal decision.

Everyone in the courtroom, in my view, was trying to tell me what to do. Even when the arguments were being made by the lawyers who were supposed to be 'on my side', it angered me that so many people were discussing my life and what I should do with my body. Not one of these people knew me personally. It was just a job to them, I felt. I was just a case study. I felt my voice was getting lost, like I was invisible.

The media attention had succeeded in attracting even more people to the quayside. From inside the courtroom, we could hear the protesters roaring their slogans over the noise of the busy traffic. The group of 'pro-choice' supporters was still smaller than the number of those who were 'pro-life'. To make up for this, they had brought huge banners supporting me and my right to decide.

Every so often the groups would start shouting at each other from either side of the public entrance, although most of the time they were happy enough to wave their placards, hoping for some supportive beeps from the passing traffic. When the noise got too loud, the judge's assistant would slam the large sash windows of the courtroom shut, making the atmosphere inside even more stifling.

My solicitor suggested it might be better if I didn't go outside for lunch and instead ate in the courts complex. My mam and my boyfriend went to get some tea and sandwiches at the café in the basement. As I sat on my own on a low wall in the courtyard waiting for them, I saw an old man coming towards me. He was dressed in black and had white hair, and at first I thought he might have a kind word to say to me. As he got closer, however, I noticed a manic look in his eyes and a crucifix and Bible in his hands.

The man approached me and started muttering – I think he may have been reciting prayers, but it sounded like gibberish. I was terrified and didn't want to talk to him but that just made him more agitated. He started muttering in a louder voice, waving the crucifix above my head. I could just about make out the words 'Satan' and 'murderer'. He took out his rosary beads and began praying over me more intensely, calling me evil. I looked around frantically for help, until I spotted my solicitor across the yard. Conor quickly signalled a security guard, who escorted the man away from me, still muttering and chanting. It makes me angry and upset for my younger self to think of that moment. It's as if I am outside my body, looking down on the scene as an observer, watching this old man praying over a scared young girl with a little bump.

After lunch, the court heard the social worker's response

to what I had told my solicitor, and his version of events was read out to the court. He said the social work team had been making plans to support me and my mother with the baby as soon as they found out I was pregnant. After the results of my scan, he said, the response of everyone in the HSE was to provide emotional support for me. He was not happy that I had claimed he was not supportive.

In his view, the meeting he had with me was calm. He said he was sympathetic but that he had told me he might have to take legal steps if I went ahead with my plan to go to England. He said he had told me and my boyfriend's mother that he would have to take legal advice, as there were 'complex legal questions'. He strongly denied that he had ever suggested I should be admitted to the psychiatric hospital to try to force me to continue with my pregnancy. He said it had never crossed his mind that I should be admitted to hospital – he was surprised when the psychiatrist suggested it, and he had sought clarity from him. He also said he believed my wishes about what I wanted to do had changed and that I myself had discussed continuing with the pregnancy. He said everyone in the HSE had every sympathy for my position and were 'most anxious' to offer 'every support' they could.

When my lawyers told me what he had said, I hit the roof. He may have believed he was being supportive, but that was not how I felt about the approach he took. I believed he had also taken my own words out of context again. He had asked me what I would do if I lost my legal case, and it was in that context that I had told him I would have to continue with the pregnancy.

It was true, however, that as the case went on I was becoming more unsure about what I wanted or what the best option was for me. I was second-guessing myself, thinking *what have I done?* Continuing to full term with this pregnancy was not something I wanted. I just didn't know if I wanted an abortion like the ones I had read about either. I was torturing myself most nights watching videos and reading articles about abortion on the internet. Maybe I could carry her after all? Should I? Might I be able to do it?

I didn't know how to tell people what was going on inside my head. After all, I thought, I had caused mayhem and the whole country knew about my case – I couldn't now turn around and say I didn't want to do any of it! I kept quiet and hoped the right thing to do for me and for my baby would become clear to me.

My lawyers told me that the legal team representing the state was not fighting against me. The state had told the court that, in its view, the HSE had no power at all to stop me from travelling. Towards the end of a very intense day of arguing in court, as I sat at the back, trying to stop my attention from wandering, I suddenly heard Mr Fitzsimons say, 'Why are we here?' I thought that was a pretty good question. The state could order the HSE to do anything, he said. It could tell the HSE to allow me to travel. If it was really its view that the HSE didn't have the power to stop me, then what were we all doing in court? He said I was in court with five legal teams, enduring a process that seemed entirely unnecessary. I agreed completely with him. I felt exhausted and emotional and couldn't wait to get back to Drogheda to get some rest.

Back at my boyfriend's house, we got ready to watch the news to try and make sense of everything that had happened that day. It was hard to pay attention for hours in a hot, stuffy courtroom, listening to people speaking in legal terms I didn't fully understand. A lot of the time I completely zoned out.

During that day, the court had heard further details about the care orders and about how my relationship with my mother had broken down. There was no doubt Mam and I had been having terrible arguments, including the one on the night when I had swallowed the tablets. But I knew she wasn't herself when those things happened. I knew she was struggling.

I have such a clear picture of that evening still in my mind – where I was, who I was with: my boyfriend, his mother, his brothers and me, all gathered around the telly, the volume turned up. The presenter on the main national evening news introduced a live report on my case from outside the Four Courts. Then the reporter, speaking from outside the courts, told the whole country about my relationship with my mother and about the reasons I was in care.

I stared at the screen in horror. I had been told my case was important and significant. My lawyers had told me the arguments in court were serious and worthy, that they were about the constitution, that the outcome would affect many other people. But all I could hear on the television was our private and personal business being relayed to the nation. That was the moment I lost all sense of self-worth – my entire identity crumbled in the space of a two-minute news report. I wanted the ground to swallow me up, I was just so ashamed.

I had spent my life, since I was 12 years old, trying to hide what was really going on and putting on my best face for the world. I made sure I dressed right and looked the part, whatever it was I was doing. Even when we were homeless, even in the women's refuge, I made sure no one could tell what was happening in our lives by looking at me. A teenager never wants to stand out for the wrong reasons. I never wanted anyone to know anything bad was going on in my life. But now my personal life – every bit of our dirty laundry – was being broadcast to the country all over the national news. I felt raw, naked and embarrassed.

I had told social workers about what was going on in my life because I was looking for help. I can be very expressive, and of course I had downplayed my own part in the rows my mother and I had. What I had told them about our arguments had not been meant for anyone else's ears. My words were never meant to harm anyone, let alone my own mother. Now, I felt they were using what I had said, in court, to show my mam in a bad light and demonstrate that she wasn't a suitable person to have a say in what happened to me. She was still my mam, and I knew she cared about me. But our relationship, which had been more strained than ever in the days since the court case had begun, was breaking apart. Mam was already fighting hard against her own demons. She presumed that I had told lies about her to the social workers. I accused her of selling stories to the newspapers. I couldn't believe that I was in a place where I was accusing my own mother of trying to destroy me. We lost all sense of connection with each other, and I didn't know if we would ever get it back.

The things that were being said about me, and the shame and embarrassment I felt, became my obsession, even more so than what was going on in the case. I got up in the morning and went straight to the local shop to buy the papers and read the stories before anyone else did. It felt as if I was getting ready for a battle every day – I wanted to know what was being said so I could fight back. I lost trust in everyone, and I felt everyone was against me.

I had to have regular scans and check-ups while the court case was going on. I started to become paranoid about the doctors in hospital, the radiographers doing the scans. Were they treating me as a patient or were they trying to help the lawyers for the other side? If I talked to a counsellor, would my words be read out in court? I didn't trust my friends or neighbours. If they asked how I was, I assumed they were looking for gossip.

A woman my mother knew who came to court with her on many of the days turned out to be a strong supporter of the pro-life campaign and was praying I would lose the case. On another occasion, I was approached by a woman who started talking to me all about the case and encouraged me to talk to her. I found out later that she was writing for a pro-life magazine. I didn't know who was who any more and if there was anyone at all I could trust.

I felt sicker with every passing day, and I found it harder than ever to concentrate. My solicitor had told me there would be no need for me to get into the witness box, as it was not that type of case. These kinds of cases, he explained, were decided on the submissions presented in court, which were in turn based on the documents – there was no need to give evidence. He thought I would be comforted by the fact that I wouldn't have to speak in court in front of everyone else. But to me, it meant I was voiceless and powerless. I wanted to scream but I didn't think it would make any difference.

5

DECISION TIME

Ooof! What was that? We were in a taxi, on our way to court, when I felt a strange sensation in my tummy. I remember how it felt, even now. I can even remember exactly where we were as it happened. We had just set off and were on the road beside the bus station in Drogheda.

I was now around 18 weeks pregnant, and my small size meant my pregnancy had become very noticeable. Over the week we had spent in court, I had gone from having a small, barely there bump to a very obvious swollen belly.

This feeling seemed to be coming from inside my stomach. There it was again! It was like a little flutter, like something was moving. In that instant, everything in my mind shifted. I turned in shock to my boyfriend and asked him to put his hand on my belly. The flutters were so gentle that he couldn't feel anything at first. But I could. My baby girl was in there, moving around. Suddenly, his face lit up. Just for a second, he felt her too. We were laughing and then, within seconds, I was sobbing. The poor taxi driver didn't know what was happening.

I had never wanted to feel those movements. That was the whole point of what we were doing. I hadn't ever wanted to build a connection with a baby who was never going to live. I dreaded the thought of carrying a baby to term only to lose her within a couple of days, at the very most. I had told the psychiatrist who evaluated me that this would be pointless. I had told my solicitor it was inhumane.

The delicate flutters reminded me of the severity of the situation I was now in. I couldn't pretend any more – this wasn't the monster or the alien I had imagined. This was my baby, kicking her little legs, turning somersaults in my tummy, saying hello in the only way she would ever be able to.

It was now Friday 4 May, almost two weeks since I had found out my baby was not going to survive. When the court case got underway that morning, even though I didn't fully understand what the lawyers were talking about, I sensed a slightly different atmosphere in the courtroom. The main barrister for the HSE seemed to be doing a lot of the talking, and he was also being asked a lot of questions by the judge. At one point, the judge asked him if the HSE thought it would be in my best interests to travel to the UK. That, he told them, was the basic question they had to answer.

I had really warmed to the judge. He was the person farthest away from me in the courtroom. I had made eye contact with him only once so far, but the questions he asked made me feel that he could see my point of view. He told the HSE legal team there was a 'core human issue here', and he reminded them that 'time was of the essence'. At last! Someone understood what was going on. I could not sit there for ever with my growing, fluttering baby bump, listening to lawyers talk and talk.

As far as I could tell, the HSE seemed to be under a bit of pressure. There was a lot of discussion about my passport. The HSE barrister told the court that my social worker had contacted the passport office before the case began. He had warned them that the HSE was not giving consent for my trip to the UK and tried to stop a new passport being issued to me. This was the first time the judge had been told this had happened.

I sat up a little straighter and began to take more notice as I realised the exchanges between the judge and this barrister were getting more tense. 'What was the HSE meant to do?' I heard the barrister ask as he urged the court to consider the position the HSE had found themselves in. He said the HSE had a lot of children in their care – my case could have implications for all of them if the HSE did not act within the law.

I could feel myself becoming emotional again, but this time I was angry, not upset. My baby was going to die. I was 17 years old, I had been forced to get involved in this legal battle with my life on public view, and here the HSE was, feeling sorry for themselves! I heard the barrister go on to tell the judge that the HSE hadn't 'cooked up a strategy' to stop me travelling. They weren't being 'heartless', he said. He asked what they were supposed to do in a situation where they believed I couldn't legally travel and I had said I was going to go.

It had become clear that the HSE's position was that a child who was in care could not travel abroad for a medical procedure without consent from the court that had made the care order. Their lawyers told the judge they did not believe a child in care could just leave the country and put herself out of the HSE's care, even if only for a limited period of time. The judge asked them what I realised afterwards was an important question – why hadn't they asked the district court for consent for me to travel *before* they contacted the Gardaí and the passport office to try to stop me? The lawyer for the HSE said they had found themselves in an awkward situation. They couldn't help me have an abortion, according to the law. And they might have been criticised if they had let me go abroad while I was the subject of a care order.

There was a lot of discussion during the day about the district court. I understood it was a lower, less important court where more ordinary, everyday issues were dealt with.

It was where the original orders, putting me into care in the first place, had been made. I was extremely confused about why everyone was spending so much time talking about going back there, but when the hearing ended for the day, my lawyers tried to explain what was going on to me.

It appeared the HSE had identified a way that they thought this whole situation could be brought to an end. They had told the judge that, as long as certain conditions were met, they were prepared to take the view that it would not be in my best interests to stop me from travelling. The conditions were that they wanted the district court to be satisfied it was legal for me to go, they wanted to be sure I had thought through my decision and had counselling, and they wanted to be sure my mother was continuing to support me.

It was not surprising that the HSE were trying to find a way of resolving the issues. The details being revealed in court had caused me soul-destroying shame and upset, but they were also embarrassing for the HSE, who were being criticised by some for their position. Even in the courtroom, they were the odd ones out among the five legal teams. The lawyers for everyone else had said I did not need permission from any court to travel.

The worried-looking health officials in suits standing around the courtroom hated media attention and wanted the case to end almost as much as I did. I could have made it easier for everyone by agreeing that I was suicidal. That would have made it more straightforward for the HSE to support my decision. But it was clear that it was not going to be possible to make my case fit the kind of abortion that was acceptable under Irish law. The HSE's plan was to go back to the district court. They said that if the judge who had made my care order agreed that I could travel to the UK, then it could all be over.

In fairness, my lawyers explained, the HSE's experienced lawyers in court realised the decisions to contact the Gardaí and the passport office were difficult to defend legally, and they had not tried to do so. The HSE's position had changed since the first letter to my solicitor, where they claimed they could intervene to stop me going. This could be a way of making things right and bringing the whole thing to a close in the quickest way possible. The High Court case would end without the judge having to make a long ruling on difficult issues, and we could get on with what we had to do.

My boyfriend, my mother and I sat in the corridor outside the courtroom that Friday evening, waiting while the lawyers decided what to do next. They huddled in groups and made a lot of phone calls. Finally, it was decided. The district-court judge had agreed to hold an emergency sitting of his court the following day – on the Saturday of a bank holiday weekend! At that sitting, the HSE would ask him if I could have permission to travel to the UK.

I know my legal team were trying to explain the proceedings to me. The problem was that I couldn't understand the issues properly – and I was too proud to tell them that. I don't think they fully appreciated how young I was, how uneducated I was and how little I knew about the world. I was also afraid to admit how much I didn't understand about the case. These were all educated people – they'd all studied law; they knew what they were doing. I was embarrassed, and for once I was worried I'd look stupid if I kept asking questions.

My mother's hearing difficulties stopped her from understanding a lot of what was going on as well. She found out later that one of the people who often came to court with her, who was supposed to help her, was not telling her everything that was happening – perhaps because of her own views on abortion, perhaps because, just like the rest of us, she found it all difficult to understand.

I felt as if I was expected to be delighted, and I was slightly hopeful that the whole legal nightmare might be finished the following day. But another part of me felt like no one wanted to deal with my case. I thought I was being pawned off, back to another judge, just as I had been moved around throughout my teenage years. In my childish way, I presumed that the High Court judge had had enough of the case and was trying to find someone else to deal with the situation.

Only the faint hope that this could all end quickly gave me the energy to go on.

The district-court hearing was just half an hour's drive from us in the neighbouring town of Dundalk. My lawyers told me that because this hearing was connected to the order putting me into care it would be in private, meaning no members of the public or the media would be allowed to attend, which was a relief to all of us. We didn't expect it to last too long.

The hearing was, to me, quite surreal. The HSE now seemed to be on my side. They were the ones asking the district-court judge for a decision about whether or not it would be legal for me to travel to the UK. They were the ones asking for an order to allow me to go and making the argument that it would not be in my best interests to stop me travelling.

My own lawyers as well as the lawyers for the state argued that no court order was necessary. Their position was that I had a right to travel and it would not be against the law for me to go.

At lunchtime, we headed into Dundalk town for something to eat. While walking through the town, Mam was approached by a journalist trying to find out what had happened in court. My mam refused to talk to them, even refusing to actually say the words 'no comment'. My boyfriend and I were freaked out by more unwanted media attention. We jumped into a shop and stayed there until the coast was clear. The arguments in court continued after lunchtime, and we then had to wait for the judge to make up his mind.

As the judge, Flann Brennan, started to give his decision, it became clear the case had not gone the way either we or the HSE had hoped. He talked about the constitution and the protection of the unborn. He mentioned another previous controversial case, involving yet another young girl, this one known as 'Miss C'. Miss C was only 13 when she was raped and became pregnant. She was also in the temporary care of social services, and her parents did not want her to travel for an abortion. The High Court ruled she could travel after hearing she was suicidal, but during his ruling the judge had made a comment that the court should not be turned into 'some form of licensing authority for abortions'. Judge Brennan, in my case, referred to that comment, and he said that granting the order the HSE wanted would be a failure by him to 'respect, defend and vindicate the rights of the unborn'. It would be improper and unlawful he said. He refused to do it.

The HSE said they would be challenging his decision, but I left the courthouse utterly deflated. Another exhausting day in court had come to nothing.

We returned to the High Court on Monday, where a summary of what had happened at the weekend was given to the judge in public. The HSE had actually already gone back to the judge the previous day to formally challenge the district court's decision, but we had not needed to be present for that.

The day dragged on with teams for the state and for the 'unborn' making long, detailed submissions to the court. I still found it crazy that the baby inside me had her own lawyers, but my legal team explained that this was because of the special protection in the constitution for the 'unborn'. Lawyers had to make arguments on her behalf and make sure she got that protection in court.

The lawyer representing my unborn baby told the court the fact that she had no brain and could not survive after birth was 'irrelevant'. She was a live foetus, he said, and her right to life was still entitled to the protection granted by the constitution. I sank lower into my seat. The possibility that had been raised by my lawyers of having the procedure I wanted in my own country was rapidly disappearing. How could her condition be irrelevant?

Once again, the judge intervened. This wasn't a case about people with disabilities or even about a child with severe neurological difficulties, he said. 'The undisputed evidence is that this baby will not live, and that is what we are dealing with,' he said, his sad words hanging heavy in the stale courtroom air. I had now been dealing with this reality for a fortnight. Why were these supposedly clever people finding this simple truth so difficult to understand?

I looked down at the sheaf of papers on my knee. Earlier, I'd been approached in the corridor by a young woman. She smiled at me and handed me a folder full of lined A4 sheets of paper. 'We just wanted to show you we support you,' she said, walking away quickly before I had a chance to say anything. Inside the folder, there were dozens of pages with a signature on every line, hundreds of them. I was stunned by the gesture and I was comforted to look through the sheets of paper as I sat in court. Each of those signatures meant a lot to me.

Despite his submissions on the right to life of my unborn child, the same lawyer also admitted that I had a right to travel and could not be stopped. Another senior lawyer, who was representing the state, told the judge that even though I was under 18, I still had rights, and I didn't suddenly get those rights on my 18th birthday. He said Ireland was a free country, and there was no law preventing a 17-year-old girl from travelling. I did not feel at all free, though. I felt trapped and utterly despairing. My belly was huge and my ankles were swollen. I looked over at my boyfriend, and we decided to leave before the court finished for the day.

We got up and walked out of court. As usual, I kept my head down so I wouldn't see the dozens of pairs of curious eyes turn towards us, eager to see what Miss D looked like or how big her bump was now. I was starting to lose energy and all hope. My doctors had told me there was a risk my baby would start to deteriorate inside me and could possibly poison my system. Because there's no skull, any brain tissue that is present in a baby with the kind of anencephaly my baby had comes into direct contact with the amniotic fluid and is slowly destroyed during the pregnancy. My bump was already much bigger than it should have been for a person of my age and at my stage of a first pregnancy. The doctors said this was due to there being too much amniotic fluid – a further complication of being pregnant with a baby with this condition.

I felt uncomfortable and nauseous all the time, and I had become resigned to my fate. It looked like it would never, ever end. I would have to continue to carry her, sitting on a hard wooden bench, listening to the endless hours of legal wrangling, all the way to 40 weeks, whatever the cost of that to my mental or physical health. I'd lost faith in there ever being a decision. I felt like I was in an endless game of tug of war. I was in the middle of the rope, slowly being pulled apart.

It was shortly after 5 p.m. that same Monday evening when my solicitor rang. Apparently, the lawyers had finally stopped arguing, and the judge was going to give his decision soon. The HSE had tried to get him to give it immediately, my solicitor said, due to the stress I was under, but the judge told them he wasn't going to do that as he wanted to consider it carefully. We would have to wait for a day and a half until he was ready. I didn't really care. I'd had enough. What did one more day or two matter? What was the point of it all anyway? It's not as if I'd be cheering and clapping or drinking champagne if he ruled in my favour. Whatever the outcome, the whole thing was disgracefully, horribly sad.

I was due to have a scan the following day. These had become routine now, but I got more and more emotional each time. The nurse applied the gel and rubbed the probe over my stomach. The image of my little girl appeared on the screen, her legs kicking, her heart still beating away. I couldn't stop sobbing. She looked like my perfect baby, except for the absence of a clear image where I knew her skull should be. 'I'm sorry,' the nurse said quietly. My boyfriend held my hand tightly as I cried. There was nothing any of us could say.

I spent the rest of the day lying on the couch, flicking through television channels, as my baby kicked inside me. I didn't want to see anyone or speak to anyone. My boyfriend's family tiptoed around me, not knowing what to do. While I lay there, I made a decision – I was not going back to that courtroom. I was too ill in my body and in my mind to listen to any more of it. I didn't want to go; I didn't want to hear what the judge had to say. I didn't want everyone looking at me trying to work out my reaction.

The judge's ruling was due at 2 p.m. on Wednesday 9 May. At around midday, my mam rang me. 'Are you sure you won't come?' she asked. I was positive. I was mentally and physically exhausted, and I was done with the court. My boyfriend was, of course, delighted that I wasn't dragging him back there. We got a taxi to the B&B instead to gather some of my things.

Just after 4 p.m. my phone rang. I looked at my boyfriend as I answered. It was Conor. He didn't waste any time. 'Amy, it's over,' he said. 'You've won – the judge says you can go.' I dropped the phone and sank to the floor. Was that it? Was that what all this fighting was about? To give me the right to do something that absolutely had to be done anyway? There was no jumping for joy.

My mam rang me minutes later and told me the judge had praised my 'maturity and integrity'. Newspaper reports of the hearing the following day described her as smiling proudly when he said that. The judge made it clear that I was not suicidal. He said I could have lied about this but, instead, I had shown courage and determination.

Judge McKechnie's words gave me great comfort at that time and in the years since. He seemed to have more compassion and empathy for me and for my family than anyone else. He saw me as a real person, not just as a symbol of an issue that had to be argued about. For a High Court judge to say those things about me – a teenager in the care of social services – it felt as good to me as if I had been praised by the President of Ireland.

My mam, of course, wanted to point out the great things the judge had also said about her. He suggested that if she continued the way she was going there would be no repeat of what he described as 'the incident' that had led to me being taken into care. She was delighted that he didn't discuss our relationship too extensively and had not allowed her name to be blackened by the evidence outlined in court.

I saw some newspaper headlines afterwards, and over the years I discussed the case with others occasionally. But that really is as much as I knew about the details of the ruling. The first time I ever read the judge's decision in full was just a few months ago while in the process of writing my story.

There are no copies of the judgment in any legal textbook or on the website of the Courts' Service, which provides a link to all the other rulings given by the High Court. My solicitor never gave me a copy and, it turned out, he had never received one himself. The only record of Mr Justice McKechnie's decision in my case was the one taken by the court stenographer, who was furiously trying to keep up with his words in the court that Wednesday afternoon. Her draft copy had been placed into the court file and, for some reason, it had been forgotten about. Maybe because there was no appeal and no further legal action, it stayed in that file, untouched, in an office in the Four Courts until a documentary team making a programme about me was given access to it in 2019. Even then, no one realised that I had never seen or fully understood what was in it. And it was many more months before I got to read it.

When I finally read it, as an older, wiser woman, I was blown away by it and wished I had seen it years ago. All 65 pages were full of compassion – for me, for my mother and for the situation we had found ourselves in. More than that, knowing how badly we had been affected by our personal details being aired in court, it seemed as if the judgment tried to protect us.

The judge deliberately didn't get into all the details of my relationship with my mother when he suggested the situation between us was improving and the incident that led to me being taken into care was unlikely to be repeated. Importantly for me, he stated very clearly that I was entirely blameless for what had happened.

'Blameless' – that word. I hadn't realised how much I needed to see it, even after more than a decade. It was nothing to do with me. I needed to believe that. Despite the fact that

I had never spoken a word to him, I felt the judge heard my voice through the words of my lawyers. He had been able to put himself in my shoes and knew how much I needed to be told I was not to blame.

Judge McKechnie had been very late coming into court to read out his ruling that afternoon, I was told, something that made me like him even more. My mother described how he rushed into court after 3 p.m., over an hour behind schedule, carrying a pile of handwritten foolscap papers, looking more like an eccentric professor than ever.

He started off by saying immediately that there was nothing to stop me travelling to the UK to terminate my pregnancy. He wanted that to be clear to me from the very beginning before he got into all the legal reasons. Even though I wasn't in court, I was grateful to him for being so considerate of me and trying to make sure I would understand. He went on to recognise what he described as the 'sheer awfulness of the situation' in which I found myself, 'without fault or neglect' on my part. When I read these words for the first time it was with a great sense of relief. Why hadn't I understood that none of this was my fault – that I hadn't done anything wrong?

He set out in detail the condition my baby was suffering from. He said he knew this was distressing but he felt it was necessary to describe it, and I'm glad he did. This was detail I hadn't really grasped before. I had watched videos and seen images, but I hadn't fully understood how deeply hopeless the diagnosis of anencephaly was. Something else I hadn't understood was that carrying her to full term could have had serious implications for my own health.

The judge noted the views of a consultant obstetrician and gynaecologist at one of the main Dublin maternity hospitals who had looked at my scan. She reported that the risks of continuing with a pregnancy like mine, at my young age, included preeclampsia and possible haemorrhage. Delivering the baby could be difficult and distressing as it got bigger, she said, and there was a risk of requiring a caesarean section. Her report said that some women who were pregnant with such a baby valued the experience of carrying it and giving birth to it. Others, however, like me, found such a prospect 'simply unbearable'.

The judge also quoted a study showing that when such pregnancies are allowed to go to full term they are associated with high complication rates without any benefit to the mothers. My baby, he said, was 'destined not to live'.

A further line in his judgment helped to ease the darkest thoughts that had been swirling around my mind since April 2007. Regretfully and tragically, the judge said, 'nature has got this wrong and has malperformed as it does from time to time with every stage of human development'. He described what had happened as 'an aberration of nature'.

I had felt for years, since I first started reading about anencephaly, that this was all somehow my fault. I hadn't taken my folic acid; I hadn't looked after my health well enough. From the minute I got the diagnosis, I had agonised, as every mother does, about what I could have done differently to prevent it. Now I started to be able to believe that perhaps my baby's situation hadn't been caused by my own actions or by not living as healthily as I 'should' have been.

The judge said the case was not about abortion: it was about the right to travel. Just because the reason I wanted to travel was to terminate a pregnancy, that didn't turn it into an abortion case. He also said the case was most definitely not about trying to end the existence of a foetus who suffered from even the most severe form of disability. It had no impact on children like that, he said, whether they were born or unborn. The baby in this case was destined to die, even with all the medical assistance and love she could be given.

I wished I had been able to print out his words back in 2007. I could have made my own placard to show those protesters outside the court. I fantasised about waving it at the old man in the cloth cap and his colleagues who were so quick to judge me.

Judge McKechnie praised my 'courage, integrity and maturity' as well as my 'sound moral judgment' for refusing the temptation to commit perjury and lie about being suicidal.

At the same time, he strongly criticised the HSE. I couldn't help thinking that if I had seen this judgment back in 2007, or if I had fully taken in how comprehensive this criticism was, other events later on could have worked out differently.

The judge ruled that it was likely from the evidence he had heard and the correspondence he had seen that the HSE at first took the view that I needed their permission to travel. Their initial position was that I couldn't go anywhere without that consent and that they could intervene to prevent me going. It was the HSE's view that they could use the full force of the state to stop me if necessary.

At the same time, the HSE also decided that the district court had to give its consent before I went anywhere. The judge described this as running two horses, 'but with a firm grip on both'. Either way, he said, the HSE had control over my destiny, but, the judge said, nowhere did they express any view at all about what might actually be best for me.

Judge McKechnie described this as a 'most crucial issue' and one that should have been addressed by the HSE before any court proceedings. He said he was 'most surprised' at the lack of any decision by the HSE about what was in my best interests. The judge believed the HSE tried to 'shoehorn' my case into a situation like the X case, where the young girl who was pregnant was also suicidal. They were trying to avoid having to make any potentially controversial decision and overconcentrated on trying to classify me as suicidal. He said the HSE had lost sight of their crucial function in relation to my welfare and failed to have regard to my wishes.

His criticism of the HSE could not have been any clearer. He said it was 'quite wrong' for them to tell me that I couldn't go to the UK without a court order permitting it. My social worker's decision to contact the Gardaí to tell them that I had to be prevented from travelling was 'without foundation either in fact or in law'. The immediate response from the garda superintendent that they had no power to do this was, the judge said, correct. He praised the HSE for not trying to stand over this during the court case and for changing their position, leading them to eventually make the application to the district court asking it to allow me to go.

The judge found the situation in relation to my passport 'unacceptable'. He said the social worker, in his first affidavit submitted to the court, had not mentioned that he had written to the passport office, telling them the HSE did not consent to a passport being issued to me. This had been done before my court case but was first mentioned to the judge several days after the case started. Judge McKechnie said he had not been given an acceptable explanation for this.

He pointed out that the HSE had the right to give consent for a passport for a child to travel for emergency treatment only if the child was in permanent care. I was not. There was an interim order only in place in my case. In fact, the HSE had no power at all to consent to a passport for me or to tell the passport office that they didn't consent. There was nothing in the legislation governing childcare that could stop a child in care travelling to the UK to terminate a pregnancy. And there was nothing giving the HSE the type of control they tried to have over me.

The judge said the HSE was obliged under the law to promote the welfare of children and to give consideration to the wishes of the child. He reminded everyone that I was 17, that my welfare was paramount and that my mother was supporting me. Even though I was in care, my mother still had rights, and she was capable of exercising her own rights to promote my welfare.

Finally, the judge said what many people had believed from the start: the right to travel took precedence over the rights of the unborn. Following the case involving the suicidal young girl in 1992, the Irish government had held a further referendum on abortion that same year. The people voted for a change to the constitution ensuring the right to life of the unborn did not limit the right to travel in and out of the state. I had always had this right. Judge McKechnie clarified that being a teenager in care did not take this right away from me. The HSE had never had any power to attempt to stop me leaving.

I read the whole judgment over one weekend. I couldn't tear myself away from it. When I finished the last page, I was in shock. It was stunning to me, so many years on, to read these words and to understand them. More than anything, once the shock faded, it stirred up a fresh anger in me. How could all this have happened to a 17-year-old girl? I felt as if I was reading about someone else's story. I felt so sorry for that girl, and I admired the fact that she had survived this ordeal. But I also wondered why no one had shouted stop. Why did the people who were supposed to care for me allow it to happen? I had been put through that incredible public trauma completely unnecessarily. So much time and so much money had been wasted, and so much damage had been done to me mentally. I had become a constitutional problem to be resolved, a case study to be argued about. My private tragedy had been exposed to the world – for what?

On the evening of 9 May 2007, however, as I sank to the floor of my bedroom after getting the news from the court, I knew none of this. I understood very little about the reasons behind the judge's decision. It had been only 16 days since my 17th birthday, since I had set off to the hospital excited to see the first images of my little baby. So much had happened since then.

I spent the rest of the evening crying uncontrollably. My boyfriend did not know what to do to comfort me. It wasn't the end. As the judge himself said, his decision did not mean my ordeal was over. The reality was much harsher. I knew that a new, much darker chapter of my life was beginning. No one was going to be able to guide me and help me with what was going to happen next. I now had choices to make, and I didn't know what to do.

6

LIVERPOOL

None of us had passports. That was part of the reason we were in this mess in the first place. Mine and my mam's had expired a long time ago, and my boyfriend had never needed one before. After the court case ended, it seemed as if the entire state was suddenly going out of its way to help us get them.

Arrangements were made to bring us to the passport office, where we were treated like VIPs. I thought we'd have to take a number and wait, but we were whisked past the queues and straight into a private room. Our photographs were taken in the office, and we were issued with the green emergency passports on the spot.

I had agreed to do an interview with a journalist who had been in court for the *Irish Independent* newspaper. The newspaper had offered me some money, which was welcome, but more importantly, I saw it as a way to get my point of view across after having to remain silent for so long. Lots of media organisations had been trying to get me to talk, but my solicitor encouraged me to accept this offer. I agreed to go along with him to meet the journalist, Dearbhail McDonald, that same day, in a hotel near the passport office.

The hotel was right across the road from Leinster House, where the parliament sat. I had been told the bar was a very popular meeting place for politicians, and I looked around hopefully. I was keen to let the politicians know exactly how Miss D herself felt about the controversial case the whole country had been talking about for almost two weeks. However, Dearbhail reminded me there was an election campaign on, which meant the TDs were out in their constituencies, campaigning, instead of being around the Dáil. It was probably just as well. Any politician we had managed to find would definitely have taken the brunt of the anger we all felt.

The newspaper needed some photographs to accompany the article. We went down to the basement of the hotel, and my boyfriend and I held hands and stared at each other in front of a window, for what seemed like hours, while the photographer got his shots. We felt stupid and found it hard to keep straight faces while staring at each other soppily. The photographer told us we needed to remain serious, which of course made us both want to laugh even more. He also took some photographs of me with my mother and on my own.

Our faces were blurred out in the pictures that were published in the newspaper, but I still have copies of some of the originals. When I look at the young girl in the photographs, I feel so sorry for her. She's wearing a stripey vest top, stretched over what was a pretty big bump for someone who was barely five months pregnant, as well as a grey hoodie and shapeless grey tracksuit bottoms. Her hair is scraped back from her face and tied up messily, and she isn't wearing any make-up. That was not how I normally looked. Clothes had always been so important to me. They were my armour, my way of coping and of presenting myself to the world. But the photographs show I had given up. I had put on clothes for the purpose of covering my body and that was it. My eyes looked dead. When I showed the photos to my mam, she cried.

I told the journalist everything. I said all the things I would have liked to have said in court. I talked and talked for a couple of hours. I had a few regrets, years later, about being so open and saying so much in this interview. My biggest regret was not putting on a better outfit for the photographs. But at the time, I was just so happy to have a voice. Dearbhail complimented me on how well I was putting my point of view across and how articulate I was. My boyfriend didn't say much at all – I think he was overwhelmed by the whole situation.

I explained to Dearbhail how the court case and the shame of hearing my personal details read out in court had destroyed me and my mother. I vented about how angry I was with the HSE. I told her about the scan I had had a few days previously. I told her we had picked a name for our baby and that I hoped to buy clothes small enough to bury her in. I told her about my dream that I would get to hold my baby and say goodbye to her properly. I also expressed my fears about abortion.

The article appeared on the front page of the Irish Independent the next day, Saturday 12 May. At that stage I was in the middle of a whirlwind of preparations for the trip to England – we were due to leave the following Tuesday – and I paid very little attention to the media coverage.

I had much more important things on my mind. The kind of procedure I was going to have in the UK had been distressing me deeply for weeks. I had been researching abortions from the moment I found out my baby had anencephaly. I like to know every angle of everything, and I wanted to try to understand as much as possible about this situation. I had googled for hours, through websites run by pro-life and pro-choice campaigners. I had disappeared down rabbit holes where I had seen horrific images of babies' bodies after abortion or where abortions had gone wrong. I had even watched videos of abortions being carried out.

To be honest, what I saw appalled and terrified me. I had always believed abortion was wrong – an easy opinion to have when it wasn't something I thought I'd have to consider. Now that I could feel my little baby fluttering and kicking inside me, the images of abortion I had seen began to haunt me, almost as much as the photographs I had seen of babies with anencephaly. My baby was totally there now – a real presence in my life. It didn't sit well with me to be making plans to have her removed from my body, but at the same time, I couldn't imagine continuing with the pregnancy either.

I met with an adviser from the Irish Family Planning Association in Dundalk, just as the court case was coming to an end. I longed for her to take control and tell me exactly what to do. I soon learned that, even if she had wanted to do that, legally she couldn't. Even though I could sense her compassion for me, she was bound by the law in Ireland at the time. She could only give me information about the options available to me; she couldn't advise me which one I should take or if I should take any of them. I was given a booklet and it was up to me to choose which procedure I wanted. I felt it was as cold and clinical as if I were picking a meal from a menu or an outfit from a website.

My choice was also limited by how far along I was. A purely medical abortion involving medication was only possible up to 12 weeks. At my stage of pregnancy, the normal procedure was dilation and evacuation, a combination of using suction, forceps and a D. and C. to scrape out the lining of the womb.

Of course, these procedures were anything but 'normal' in Ireland at the time. The faint hope that had been sparked in me by the suggestion my barrister had made in court about staying in my own country instead of travelling to the UK had been quickly dashed. The argument that my baby did not count as 'unborn' because she was not going to live was not one the Irish state was willing to look favourably on at that time. The judge had not made a decision on that issue in his ruling. My case, he had said, was about the right to travel, not about abortion or about what the word 'unborn' meant.

I agonised over the life-changing decision I had to make while Rosie from the Family Planning Association talked through the choices I had in front of me. She pointed out all the options, including one I had not previously known about: I could decide to be induced and give birth to my daughter. She explained that this procedure, sometimes called a 'compassionate induction', was used much more rarely, but it was sometimes chosen by parents in cases where the foetus could not survive. It would be much riskier for me. It meant I would have to go through labour and I would suffer more side effects. But I was much more at peace with this plan. I decided this would be the best way for me to show respect to my baby. I wanted to push her out. I wanted to give birth to her. More than anything, I wanted her to have a birth certificate and to hold her as she took a breath.

Rosie knew this, and before I left her office she said she wanted to give me something. She handed me a tiny blue elephant for my baby and told me to make sure I brought it to England with me. I was scared and I wanted her to come with me. I also wished I had met her earlier on in the process. She might not have been able to tell me exactly what to do, but talking through my options with her at an earlier stage might have spared me hours of endless, useless guilt about my choice.

The obstetrician who had evaluated me for my court case had written in her report that the decision I had to make was distressing and deeply personal. She also said it was vital that I received the best of medical and psychological care during and after the delivery of the baby, whether that happened at 18 weeks or 38 weeks. I should have paid more heed to her words, but I didn't think about the possible complications or about the effect it would all have on me.

I remember vividly having to make the crucial decision about how my baby would come out of my body. I don't recall being given options about what would happen afterwards or getting advice on how I would feel and how long it would take me to recover. I'm not sure those who were booking my flights understood the procedure I was going to have or thought very deeply about the aftermath, either. I'm not sure I understood it properly myself. I was given an envelope with our flight and accommodation details. It was like a race to get me to England, get it done and get home. I felt I had no control over the situation or how things were done. I presumed that once the baby was gone I could get back to 'normal' life – not that much about my life was normal at that time.

Before we left for the UK, my boyfriend and I headed into town. I wanted to buy the things I would need for the hospital, and my boyfriend had asked me to get him some new clothes for the trip. Part of me was still a silly little teenager, almost excited to be getting a few new pairs of pyjamas and knickers. I had been paid for the newspaper interview, and it was a real novelty to have some money in my pocket for the first time in months. My boyfriend got some fancy tracksuits; I saved some cash for the journey and gave some to my boyfriend's mother. She was coming with us, but she needed to make sure her other kids would be looked after while we were gone. I didn't get much for myself. I wasn't bothered with new clothes beyond a few essentials. Anyway, trying on clothes was not an option. I could barely bring myself to look at my stomach or to catch sight of myself in a mirror.

At my boyfriend's house, there was excitement in the air. Everyone was in holiday mode. We were heading to the Women's Hospital in Liverpool, much to the delight of my boyfriend's brothers. Like so many Irish people, they were all big Liverpool FC fans. The younger kids begged their mother to bring back jerseys and scarves and all kinds of other souvenirs.

My boyfriend had never been out of Ireland and this trip was a big deal for him. In fact, it was a long time since any of us had left the country. Suitcases were dragged from the top of wardrobes; there was a frantic search for any sterling anyone might have stashed away. My boyfriend's mother gathered her toiletries and chose her outfits. My own mother was doing the same in her place. All the hustle and bustle made me feel sick. This was no holiday for me.

We headed to the airport the next morning in a taxi, stopping to collect my mam on the way. I was now in extreme physical discomfort – I felt like my whole body was puffy and swollen. I had no ankles any more. As we walked through the airport doors, I was also mortified, convinced everyone was staring at me. My case had been all over the news for the past fortnight, and now here I was – a young girl standing in the airport with a bump and a suitcase and a ticket for a Liverpool-bound flight. I thought everyone would know I was Miss D on my way to England for my abortion. How could they not know?

At the check-in desk I wanted to die with shame. The woman who checked us in seemed perfectly nice, but I thought

I caught her looking me up and down, her eyes snagging for a minute on my obvious bump. We presented our emergency passports. Surely now she would know. Her expression didn't change, even though I was convinced she was judging me. It's much more likely that she had no idea who I was, or maybe she was actually looking at me with compassion. But I was paranoid and couldn't think rationally. I kept my head down and tried not to look at any of the other passengers.

I was shaking as we went through security, but the staff were particularly kind and courteous to me. At the boarding gate, the others made themselves comfortable with their takeaway coffees, sandwiches and muffins. I couldn't understand how they could eat. I ran, sobbing, to the toilets, where I stayed until it was time to board the plane.

The flight to Liverpool took less than an hour. We arrived at around 11 a.m. and settled into our hotel. I had an appointment almost immediately at the hospital. I was greeted by a doctor and nurse, who discussed what was going to happen over the next few days, before the nurse prepared me for yet another ultrasound scan.

I was used to seeing the images now, but the room fell silent as my baby appeared on the screen. Her head was just so small. I had seen many 'normal' baby scans on the internet during my obsessive googling. At five months, I knew her head should have looked much bigger than her body. With my baby, it was the other way around. The nurse squeezed my hand and gave me a kind smile. There was no doubt about my daughter's diagnosis.

Despite this, though, I had one hope left. 'I'd like her to be able to take a breath,' I told the nurse. I was young and naïve and, even faced with the scans right in front of me, showing the truth of my daughter's condition, I thought there might be some chance of a miracle. Maybe she could somehow survive. Maybe when she came out her skull would be all right after all. Maybe it was just the way she was lying in the womb. Maybe the doctors and nurses, in Dublin and here in Liverpool, had all got it wrong. The nurse just smiled again. She looked at my mother and nodded at me. The medical staff could see how important this was to me, so they stayed quiet. They didn't tell me that what I was hoping for was impossible. In my anxious state, I didn't take in what the eerie quiet of the room was already telling me. Maybe I didn't want to.

I was given medication to induce the baby, and the nurse explained to me that I was to come back a couple of days later when I would hopefully be in labour. As we were leaving the hospital, we noticed a table in a corner of the reception area laid out with tiny little knitted dresses and cardigans. They looked like very small dolls' clothes. Two older ladies were sitting beside the table, knitting away. They explained to us they were making outfits for premature babies to raise money for the hospital's neonatal unit. We hadn't had any time to get any special clothes made for our baby, who was obviously going to be much smaller than an ordinary new-born. We thought maybe these would fit her. We bought two little dresses and two matching cardigans. They were the smallest sizes they had – so small it didn't seem possible that any human baby would fit into them, but we had no idea what to expect. The women wrapped up the clothes carefully for us and we headed back to the hotel.

All we could do now was wait. For the others, this meant it was time to shop, something I would normally have loved to do. We got a taxi for the short journey from the hotel to the main shopping area in Liverpool city centre. Our first stop was, of course, the Liverpool FC shop on Williamson Square. Both of our mothers gathered up jerseys, scarves and hats to bring home. Church Street nearby was the main shopping area, and we headed there afterwards. It was lined with all the big high street shops, including some that didn't have outlets in Ireland. It was the kind of street I would usually have loved to spend hours wandering around, but that day I had lost all interest. My boyfriend's mother tried to get me excited about a pair of shoes, but I couldn't face even trying them on in such circumstances.

After about half an hour, I became overwhelmingly nauseous and asked my boyfriend to bring me back to the hotel. The others returned a short while later, laden with shopping and carrying bags of food from McDonald's. The smell made me want to vomit. The tablets I had been given in the hospital were taking effect and everything tasted vile.

Later, both our mothers headed out again into the city, leaving me at the hotel with my boyfriend. He didn't want to talk about what was going on, so, mentally, I was on my own with the thoughts that were terrifying me. I had been haunted since we arrived by the idea that the doctors might be wrong. What if this was a mistake? What if our baby came out perfectly formed, but because she was being induced so early, she would be unable to survive? I felt very nervous and wondered if I was doing the right thing. It was a heavy burden to carry on my own.

Less than 48 hours later I was back in hospital to continue the induction process, and by the following morning, the contractions were starting. Liverpool Women's Hospital wasn't just a place where procedures like mine were carried out. It was a normal hospital where people went to have their babies, as well as other obstetrical and gynaecological procedures. As I was brought to my private room, I could hear the unmistakable cries of new-born babies coming from the various wards.

I was introduced to the midwives who would be minding me. One of the nurses was a woman around the same age as my older sister, and I became very attached to her. I still have a photograph of us together in my room. Every time she passed the door, she popped in to chat to me and I would share one of my chocolates with her, from the huge box of Ferrero Rocher I had brought with me to see me through the labour. She didn't realise she was doing anything special or how much it meant to me. She didn't know how her kindness carried me through the ordeal. My boyfriend and our mothers were doing the best they could. But it was the nurse's support and empathy that really kept me going and comforted me.

I think it helped that this was a situation the nurses in England, and particularly in the Liverpool Women's Hospital, were used to. They had the training and they understood the emotional trauma I was experiencing. I was not the first young woman in this situation they had dealt with, and I wouldn't be the last. My case had caused major controversy in Ireland, but here it was almost routine. For the first time since I was a little girl, I felt completely looked after.

The labour pains became more intense as the afternoon went on, and the nurse asked me if I wanted to take any pain medication. I refused. I was desperate to give my baby every chance of surviving the birth. I was adamant that I was not going to take any drugs that could harm her. If she was to have any chance of taking her first breath, I had to help her by staying away from the morphine they were offering me. I wanted her to live, and I wanted to have proof that she lived and that she was loved. Maybe in the back of my mind I was trying to prove the pro-life protesters outside court wrong and to ease my own feelings of shame and guilt. I wanted to show them that I wasn't 'killing' a child, that this wasn't really an abortion. I saw my mam exchange a glance with my boyfriend's mother. I knew they were worried about me, but I was determined to give my baby the hug and cuddle she deserved.

The pains were excruciating. My mam stayed beside me, stroking my hand and telling me it would be all right, even while I was roaring and cursing at her. On a couple of occasions, however, she left the room to take phone calls. I wondered why she was leaving me – what could be so important? Later, she told me that, while I was screaming in pain, she was getting calls from people claiming to be pro-life activists pleading with her to stop me from going ahead with the procedure. She was told there was money already in a bank account, available to support me if I didn't go through with it. Mam told them to go to hell and didn't say a word about it to me until days afterwards. I was very glad I didn't know at the time that this was going on.

After around 12 hours of pain, with very little sign of

progress, my mam stepped in and took control. She put her hand on my shoulder and told me to trust the doctors and take the morphine they wanted to give me. 'It won't hurt her, Amy,' she said. 'I promise.' As I looked into my mam's eyes, I knew I had to trust her. My mother wasn't lying to me – she was just bending the truth a little. My boyfriend and I were probably the only people in the room who didn't know our baby had passed away. My mam had already been told there was no heartbeat. I didn't realise that was the reason everything had been so eerily quiet when I had my first scan on our arrival. It's possible I just didn't want to believe it. I'm still not sure exactly when my baby died. There are some details I'm unclear about to this day. It may be that she passed away while we were on our way to Liverpool. That makes me wonder what would have happened if we had found out she had died before we left Ireland. Would they then have performed the procedure at home, after all the controversy of the court case? Would there have been any need at all for this horror and pain in a city I didn't know?

In some ways, finding out that she had died inside me eased my guilt a little in the years afterwards. I felt it was God's way of helping me to process the situation mentally. I didn't feel that I had contributed to her death. She had already gone, and she had to come out of my body no matter what. Later, I wanted everyone to know this. I thought they might stop talking about me and linking my name to abortion, which I still felt great shame about. But even in newspaper interviews and articles about my case, I never seemed to be able to get this point across properly.

In the hospital, I was becoming more exhausted with every minute, and after my mother's intervention, I accepted all the drugs I was being offered. The physical pain eased, although I was still in mental agony. It was important for me to do this, yet I was terrified of seeing my baby.

The labour lasted for 16 hours in total, and the sensation of giving birth to my tiny little child is one I'll never forget. It was as if she just fell out into the bed, like a dead fish, onto my legs. I know that sounds horrible and to me, at 17 years old, it was horrific and extremely traumatic. And still the pain continued. The placenta had yet to come out. In my ignorance, I barely knew what that was. I was screaming and roaring in pain and in panic as I pushed out the afterbirth, which was bigger than my little baby.

As I was pushing, everyone in the room also seemed to be panicking. It was so noisy that it didn't register with me that I hadn't yet heard a baby's cry. There was shouting and running, and she was taken away from me before I got a chance to see her. Shattered, and broken-hearted, I passed out.

✤

I woke again in the early hours of Saturday morning, 19 May. My boyfriend was beside my bed, tears in his eyes. It was then I finally accepted what I'd known in my heart as I gave birth to her. Our baby was gone. She would never get a chance to take a breath. My boyfriend held my hand and spoke to me more kindly than he had ever spoken to me before. 'Amy,' he said quietly, 'do you want to see her?' Honestly, I didn't. I was scared. I had seen the pictures on the internet. I had read about what these babies could look like. He and our mothers had had a few hours to come to terms with what was going on. I was still very groggy, and I just didn't think I could do it. I started to cry. 'It's OK,' he said, 'I promise.' Gently, he helped me into a wheelchair and wheeled me towards the room adjoining mine. 'You can see her face,' he said. 'But don't look if you don't want to.'

He pushed me to the doorway, but I wouldn't go any further. I was crying and shaking. There was just too much to process. He brought me back into my own room and spoke to me kindly again, telling me it was going to be OK, telling me there was nothing to be afraid of. It took several attempts, but finally he managed to calm me down a little and wheel me into the room next door.

I already knew my daughter's name. It had been an easy decision to make. I'd chosen it almost as soon as I'd felt the first flutters. When I was a small child, I spent my time in

Almost two years old with my mam in the bathroom at the back of my grandparents' house in Rathfarnham. She had me dressed immaculately as usual, complete with coordinating shoes.

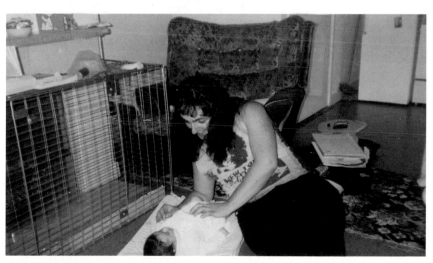

At home in Jobstown with my dad, not long after I was born. I didn't see him again until 2018.

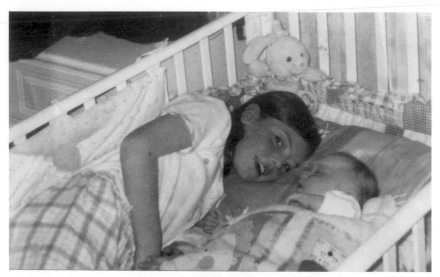

Trying to get as close as possible to my little sister Claire after her birth in 1999. I adored her.

At Leinster House in 2006 with the then Minister for Children, Brian Lenihan, representing the views of young people from around the country. (*Courtesy of the Evening Herald/Mediahuis Ireland*)

Protests outside the High Court, while my case was under way inside. You can see the two groups gathered on each side of the entrance, as well as some of the placards I found so upsetting. (© *Rolling News*)

One of the photographs taken for the *Irish Independent* at Buswells Hotel in Dublin in May 2007, on the day we got our emergency passports. It's hard to believe that sad and lost-looking girl is me. (*Courtesy of Liam Mulcahy/Irish Independent*)

In a room at Liverpool Women's Hospital on the day I was brought in to be induced. I find it difficult to look at this picture and to see in my eyes how devastated I was.

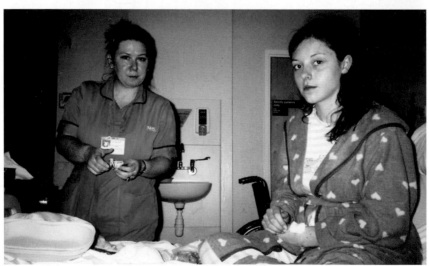

Still waiting to give birth. I was starting to feel the pain and see the reality of what was about to happen. But I was blessed to have the comfort of a nurse who was so empathetic.

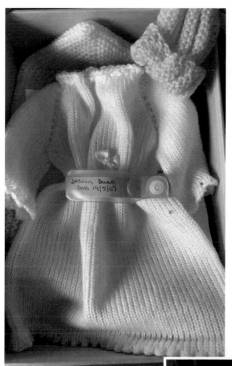

Inside the memory box made for me at the hospital. You can see Jasmine's identification bracelet and her little hat and one of the dresses we got for her. The message written inside the box read, 'With love for you always, from the League of Friends at the Liverpool Women's Hospital.' This box got me through some of my darkest days.

Jasmine's grave. I spray-painted the wreath to make it more girly and glamorous.

Dear Dad

16th July 07

I dont know why you never returned my calls last year. I am in care since febuary. I want you to know you have a grandchild, her name is Jasmine Claire

I got a scan on the day of my birthday only to find out our baby had anencephaly, a disease which meant my baby was missing her skull and the major part of her brain, I had a choice carry her to term and risk being very ill or having an abortion, my baby had no chance of survival, I was confused I wanted her so bad, anyway it was brought to the "High Court", I needed barristers, solicitors, it was huge it went 'WORLDWIDE' all over papers, Radios, telly, different countrys, My name was 'Miss D' thats to protect my identity. It went to court because I was in care + they were against abortion, in the end I won the case 75% of Ireland were on my side and chose not to have an abortion, I went to england and I got induced, I delivered my baby girl, she was so small + fragile, I was only 5 months pregnant she is beautiful at only 8 oz's she had

One of the letters I wrote to my dad after the court case, but never sent. At the end of the letter I asked him to 'please contact me'.

At the finals of the Diva Next Door modelling competition in 2013. I didn't win, but you can see how happy I was to be there. (*Courtesy of Diva Next Door and Sunday World/Mediahuis Ireland*)

With my mam and Lola, my bulldog, in early 2020. I was just starting to walk again after breaking my back. Mam and I are very close, and she has been a great support to me.

With my son, Adam. I'm so proud of the lovely boy he has become. He has been my best friend since he was born, and he has given me the strength I've needed to survive.

a bubble of believing in princesses and make-believe, magic and happy-ever-after. As I grew older, and life got tougher, I had a fantasy that someone would wave a magic wand or swoop in and save me and make it all better. The even more fantastical dream I had was that this person would be my dad. My favourite Disney princess had always been Princess Jasmine, from Aladdin. I too wanted to be whisked away on a flying carpet, away from all my troubles.

When my little sister, Claire, came along, I loved to read my fairy tales to her and tell her we would one day live happily ever after. I had always tried to look after Claire and be a second mother to her, so I wanted to name our daughter Jasmine Claire. If I wasn't going to get to be a princess, my daughter certainly would be. My boyfriend knew better than to argue with me about this. My mind was made up.

Now he guided me gently towards the cot in the centre of the room. It was an ordinary hospital cot with see-through sides, the perfect size for a normal new-born baby. In the middle of the mattress, her head covered by a pink, knitted blanket, was Jasmine. She was a dainty little creature, even smaller than a baby doll. She took up such a tiny amount of space in the cot. She had a nappy on, probably the smallest nappy you could possibly buy, but on her, it was huge.

I noticed her little feet first. Each foot was perfectly formed, although her left foot was slightly twisted from the delivery.

She had perfect little toes and tiny paper-thin nails on each one. My boyfriend encouraged me to touch her. I reached out towards her hands and her little fingers. I picked them up and looked at the miniature nails. Her whole hand could rest on the top of my little finger. Her face was covered by a corner of the blanket. I didn't yet have the courage to lift it.

I asked my boyfriend to hand me the little blue elephant that Rosie from the family planning centre had given me, and I placed it gently beside Jasmine in the cot. I noticed she was wearing a tiny lemon cardigan we had bought from the women downstairs over her miniature nappy. My boyfriend showed me the little knitted dresses we had also bought. 'They were too big,' he said. That broke me. The hurt I could see in him made it all real. I had an overwhelming sense that this wasn't a 'situation' to be managed any more. This was my little girl, and I was a mammy.

I was trying to gather up the courage to take off the blanket and pick her up. She was so exquisitely small, I was afraid I would break her. I think if I had been given more time I probably would have held her, but I was aware that the clock was ticking. It was already 6 a.m. and our flight home was booked for ten that morning.

I continue to carry a lot of anger about what happened in the aftermath of the birth. That anger has only grown stronger over the years. I don't realise how upset I still am until I start trying to talk or write about it. I think it has become harder as I get older because I can now imagine being the mother of that 17-year-old girl. If I was the parent of a child in a situation like that now, I would speak out and stop it from happening. I would put my foot down and say we weren't going anywhere until my daughter had time to recover and had spent as much time as she needed with her baby. I had only just given birth. The emotions and hormones of motherhood were washing over me, along with utter exhaustion and the after-effects of the drugs I had been given. All my feelings about that morning come down to one word – time. I should have been given more time.

Maybe the arrangements were made that way because those making them didn't fully understand the procedure I was having. Maybe it was 'just' an abortion to them and no one considered that I would need to spend time with the baby. Maybe it was pure thoughtlessness. No one took into account that I had been forced to spend days in court with Jasmine fluttering in my tummy. I had given birth to her, and now I was being torn away from her.

The whole situation was beyond my control. And those around me were equally powerless at that time, or they believed they were. Because of the situation my mother was in with the HSE, and the fact that I was under a care order, she didn't feel she had the power to challenge the decisions that were made. She felt she was seen as a mother who couldn't look after her daughter properly and had no option but to do what she was told. My boyfriend's mother was eager to get back to Dublin, but there was no reason I couldn't have stayed for even a day or two longer. Why had no one considered what it would be like for me to deliver a child and immediately get on a flight back home? It was devastating and cruel. If I had been in Ireland, I would have had as much time as I needed.

There was a gentle knock on the door and the hospital chaplain came into the room. He was a man in his fifties and he spoke with a soft Liverpool accent. 'Would you like me to bless your child?' he asked. I don't remember saying yes, but I must have nodded because a nurse picked Jasmine up and placed her in the priest's arms. As he began the blessing, I began to bawl, making noises I'd never heard coming from my mouth before. I was angry and I was jealous. This man was holding my child, and I hadn't even had a chance to hold her yet. I hadn't given him permission to hold her! I was also worried that he would damage her. He was standing there with her little thighs in his arms, and I was so scared she would break – her body was so fragile. At the same time, I didn't want him to finish his prayers. When the blessing was over, I knew it was going to be time to say goodbye. 'Amy,' my mam said quietly after a few minutes, 'we have to go.'

Afterwards, I had to ask the others what she looked like.

Everyone else got a bit more time to make peace with Jasmine's condition, to hold her and to see her face. My boyfriend, his mother, my mother, they had all seen her. I have never seen my daughter's face and it eats me alive to this day. It's something I have to carry for ever – I can never get that time back. I didn't get enough time to process the situation and to gather up the courage to look at her properly.

My mam told me, of course, that Jasmine was absolutely gorgeous and looked like the angel she was. My boyfriend's mother had a different memory. My boyfriend himself never really spoke about what she looked like. I don't think he could get the words out. All I remember was the beauty of her delicate little hands and feet. I never saw what lay beneath the blanket.

By the time we were ready to leave, Jasmine's body was already changing colour. I was still suffering from the effects of the morphine and was not really with it. I was horrified and fascinated, freaked out and broken-hearted, all at the same time. My boyfriend helped me settle back into my wheelchair and started wheeling me out of the room. That was when something inside me broke. How could I possibly leave my child alone in a hospital room? Anyone might just walk in on her. What if they were scared by her? What would they do to her?

I was asked to sign paperwork giving my consent to an autopsy. I didn't want her to have one. I didn't want her little body to be handled more than it already had been. I agreed to let them do all that was necessary, and nothing more than that. But signing the consent form made me believe that, not only was I leaving my little baby alone, but I was also leaving her to be chopped into pieces. I lost it.

I began sobbing. I tried to hold on to the walls with my fingertips, to stop the wheelchair from moving, but there was nothing I could get a grip of. As my boyfriend wheeled me past the nurses' station, I screamed at them at the top of my lungs: 'My baby! My baby! Please don't leave her on her own!' I begged the nurses to promise me that they would stay with her, that they wouldn't let anyone touch her or harm her. They tried to comfort me, tears in their own eyes. I was irrationally jealous of them – they were going to get to spend time with my child while I had to leave. I had no idea how long she'd be in that little room. I didn't know what would happen next and when, if ever, she would come home to me. The nurses tried to reassure me that she would be looked after with respect and that everything would be all right.

At the airport, I was hysterical and inconsolable. I wanted my baby so badly. Every part of me ached. I was crying, bleeding, in agony. My mother and my boyfriend helped me onto the plane and tried to settle me down. Within minutes of take-off, much to everyone's relief, I passed out again and slept for the duration of the short flight back to Ireland. I wanted to stay asleep, oblivious to everything. I couldn't take any more.

7

AFTERMATH

ack home, we gave the kids their new jerseys and scarves, their sweets and footballs. There were no more trips to court, no more consultations with lawyers. There was no longer a pregnancy. I got the feeling I was expected to get myself together and get on with my life.

Everyone was shattered and wanted the drama to come to an end. I began to feel uncomfortable in my boyfriend's house, as if I had overstayed my welcome. I was dragging myself from the couch in their house to the B&B in Slane and didn't have anywhere I felt really at home.

I discovered when I went back to the B&B that most of my stuff had disappeared. My room had been rented out to other people while I was in England, and I believed my belongings had been stored safely. But when I went to retrieve them, they couldn't be found. I lost almost everything: clothes and shoes as well as documents that were important to me, including the original reports of Jasmine's scan and diagnosis. There were other things that meant a lot to me: a half empty bottle of Jean Paul Gaultier perfume I'd been given as a present – the only perfume I owned – as well as a few bits of jewellery I'd left behind. I was distraught. There wasn't much, but these were my only possessions, beyond what I'd had in Liverpool with me. The documents and paperwork wouldn't have been of any value to anyone else and had probably just been dumped somewhere. I made a report to the guards but never got anything back.

My body was aching in every single way and my hormones were running wild. A few days after I came home, I noticed wet patches on the front of my T-shirt. My milk had come in. It was a shock to me. I hadn't expected it to happen because I had given birth to Jasmine at such an early stage in my pregnancy. I went to the doctor to get medicine to dry it up. It was another reminder that, although I was a mammy, I had no baby.

I began to turn in on myself. I spent some days in bed, curled up under the covers, not able to cry any more. I thought constantly about Jasmine and about leaving her little body in England. Inside, I was screaming for the child I had left over the water. I wanted to go back over to Liverpool, to see her face, to hold her and do all the things I didn't get the chance to do that morning. That was all I had wanted, to sit there quietly with her, just for a few hours, to come to terms with what had happened.

Closing my eyes didn't bring any relief. I was haunted by nightmares. Images of the babies with anencephaly I had seen on the internet swirled around my head, along with my memories of Jasmine's vulnerable body lying in her cot.

I thought about the paperwork I had signed and the tests that I had approved. I knew they had to be done. I thought they might help other people who had pregnancies like mine. But Jasmine was my child and I had wanted to protect her. I couldn't bear thinking of what might have been done to her body. I tried to pull myself together. There were practicalities to be dealt with and a funeral to organise.

At 17, I had been to two funerals in my entire life, and I had no idea how to plan one. It's a stressful experience for the most functional of families. For us, it brought up all kinds of emotions and arguments. Who would we ask to come? Where would the funeral be held? Could we or should we have a mass in a church? What would happen afterwards? I can't blame anyone for the confusion and stress. How could any of us have known the right way to deal with something like this?

We got in touch with the local undertaker and arrangements were finalised. I realise now that it must have been an unusual situation for them as well, but they were kind and respectful in their dealings with me as we tried to work out the logistics.

Finally, I got word that Jasmine's body would be flown into Belfast on 8 June, and we would have a funeral for her the following day, exactly three weeks after I had given birth to her.

As we waited for her body to come home, my nightmares began to intrude into my waking hours. I was consumed by horrific thoughts too graphic to speak out loud to anyone else. I worried about the effect of the flight on Jasmine's fragile little body. I imagined her body shaking around in a box, without me, her mammy, to hold her and mind her. I didn't know what arrangements would be made for her. I didn't know if the airport workers would have to open her coffin and check it before putting it on the flight. I wondered if she would be thrown in the hold by the baggage handlers – just another piece of luggage like all the others, flung around the place by some young fella, ignorant about what was inside. I worried that she wouldn't be given the respect she deserved.

I wanted to see her when she arrived home. I was still desperate to hold her and see her face. But the undertakers told me too much time had passed. We had to choose a new coffin for her, as the casket she arrived home in was too small for the crucifix I had chosen to go on the top of it. I wondered if the funeral directors would get to see her, and I was haunted by the thoughts of what they might see.

It was decided we would have a small ceremony in the funeral home before going directly to the cemetery where Jasmine would be buried. I was hurt that we were not going to have a full funeral mass or service in the church. I presumed it was because she had never taken a breath. I felt neither she nor I was considered important enough for a proper funeral to be held and that this ceremony was taking place purely to pacify me.

I felt as if I couldn't win. On one hand, I had heard pro-life protesters say that what I had done was wrong, that I had killed an innocent child, discarding her like rubbish. But now, when I wanted to honour her and give her the respect that she was due as my daughter, I wasn't allowed to have the kind of funeral she deserved because she wasn't considered to have been a living child.

On the morning of the funeral, I pulled on a pair of black trousers and a top, over my still swollen and misshapen stomach. I was a shell of a person at this stage, just about managing to function. Part of me couldn't actually believe this was happening. It was less than two months since I had first heard the word anencephaly. Now I was burying my baby. Shortly before 10 a.m., a car came to bring us to the funeral home.

My heart broke when we walked in and I saw the little white coffin. It seemed too small for the huge room, just as her body had seemed so tiny in the cot at the hospital. Chairs were arranged all around the room, ready for the usual crowds of mourners you would expect at a wake. But to me this was no ordinary funeral.

We had time on our own as a family with our mothers, to say some prayers for Jasmine before anyone else arrived. It was intimate and respectful but I felt numb. I wasn't sure what I believed in any more. Over the previous weeks, my religion had been used against me by my own country. It was tainted for me. I wondered why any God would have let this happen to me and to an innocent baby.

Mourners started to gather. Some of my teachers from Youthreach arrived and I was grateful to see them, as they were like family to me. My boyfriend's auntie walked in carrying a little teddy. 'I brought this to put on the coffin,' she told me. I was delighted she had thought of it. But at the same time, I felt jealous and annoyed that I hadn't thought of it myself. Why hadn't I brought something to comfort my own little baby? Again, I beat myself up for yet another way in which I believed I had failed my child. Everyone else seemed to know exactly what to do and I didn't have a clue.

Mam wasn't coping well. This was the one day in my life when I really needed my mammy, but she seemed to be focused purely on her own grief. She greeted some relatives and friends who had come from Dublin, and I tried to stay out of her way as much as possible while we were in the funeral home.

Around 30 people came in the end and signed the book of condolence. The local priest stood beside the coffin and said some prayers and a few decades of the rosary. I was in a daze and didn't take in much of what he said, beyond hearing him say that my baby was now an angel. The ceremony was short and peaceful, and it was comforting to have people around us.

Afterwards, we got ready to travel to the cemetery, which was just over three and a half kilometres away. I didn't know what to expect at that stage either. I had a vision of us walking slowly behind a hearse across the town. That's not what happened.

My mother, my boyfriend and I climbed into the back of a limousine, and Jasmine's tiny coffin was handed in to us to hold. I thought not enough fuss was being made about her because of the circumstances in which she had been born. I can see now a hearse would not have been necessary and I know everyone was doing their best to make sure it was all done in a respectful and dignified way. But back then, it just added to my confusion and annoyance. I felt I was expected to be grateful that I was able to have any kind of funeral at all. But I wasn't grateful then, and I'm still not. I shouldn't have had to leave the country to get the care I needed. Jasmine shouldn't have had to come home as cargo in a plane for me to bury three weeks later.

My boyfriend sat in the middle of the back seat, me and my mam on either side of him. He was holding the little coffin tight. We were both full of concern, trying to keep it as steady as possible. Although we were being driven very slowly, with every bump or sharp turn in the road we were petrified it would fall and break open. My boyfriend's knuckles were white as he gripped it firmly and clenched his jaw to try to keep his emotions under control.

The argument started around halfway to the graveyard. I can't even remember how or why it started. It's possible we had told Mam to keep still. I may have snapped at her because I was so worried about keeping the coffin from moving. Whatever happened, she took offence. While we were stopped at traffic lights, she opened the door and got out, right in the middle of the road, screaming and shouting at us. I was devastated and begged her to get back in. I couldn't believe she had made this day all about herself. She was focused on her own hurt as the mother of a daughter who had lost a child in tragic circumstances. I wanted to focus on Jasmine, and that was being taken away from me.

Mam refused to get back into the car, and we continued to the graveyard while she made her way there on foot. A small group of friends and family members were waiting at the cemetery. My boyfriend was meant to carry the coffin to the graveside, but as we got out of the car, he began sobbing. This was a man who did not show emotion easily and I was shocked. He was overwhelmed and too afraid to carry the little coffin any further and the undertakers had to take over.

The cemetery where Jasmine was to be buried is not the most picturesque of graveyards. It's a plain enough, functional field, with neat rows of graves. The plot that had been organised for us wasn't shaded by plants or trees and it didn't have any kind of view. But what was most important to me was that it was near my boyfriend's home and the parts of Drogheda where we spent our time. It would be easy for me to visit.

At the graveside, we released a white dove and I read a poem. The title was 'Kissed by an Angel' and it ended with the words: 'So, remember that I have kissed your heart, and I love you more than you can see. An angel for you to love in heaven. This is how it was meant to be.' I truly believed those lines. Jasmine became my guardian angel that day, and I believe she still watches over me. But as her tiny coffin was gently lowered into the ground, talk of angels wasn't much comfort to me. I wanted to go into the grave with her. I was in turmoil, hysterical. My boyfriend, her father, was distraught and also wanted to follow her coffin into the ground.

It all ended quickly, too quickly. I was carried away, back

to the car, leaving my baby there with the gravediggers. It was like abandoning her at the hospital all over again.

As we drove away, I looked back at the simple cross marking the grave and planned what I would do for Jasmine. I had picked out a headstone – a beautiful angel, holding a heart, but I needed time to save up for it. I was determined to make the grave as pretty as it could be for my little daughter.

Afterwards, our families headed to the pub. This had been the source of many arguments in the previous week. Our immediate families had insisted that we should look after our relatives, some of whom had come from Dublin, by having a drink and something to eat in the local pub. I thought this was disrespectful to my baby. I know there are certain rituals around death, but this had been such a bizarre, unnatural event that I couldn't see the need for a get-together of any kind. It was not how I wanted to deal with my feelings at that time.

Neither my boyfriend nor I were big drinkers, and we didn't want to get drunk. It wasn't a question of being able to celebrate a long life well lived. We were mourning the loss of a life that never had a chance. We joined our families for an orange juice and left after less than an hour.

My only comfort in the days afterwards came from a gift Liverpool Women's Hospital had given me just before I left. A charity based at the hospital put together a memory box of keepsakes. Their experience of dealing with women in the traumatic situation I was in again shone through. They knew what would help me come to terms with Jasmine's loss, even when I didn't know myself. Inside the lid of the box was an inscription saying it was sent with love for me, 'always'. I couldn't believe the care they had taken over what they had put into it.

It turned out that while I had been asleep after giving birth to Jasmine, the nurses had been busily working away, knowing I would have to leave within hours. They had taken prints of her tiny hands and feet and placed them on a laminated card with her full name as well as the date she was delivered. Each footprint was just three centimetres long. They took photographs of Jasmine for me after I woke up and printed them before we left. She was just as I remembered her, the pink knitted blanket covering her face and the little blue elephant given to me by Rosie in the Family Planning Association by her side. I would never, in a million years, have considered taking photographs, but the nurses told me I would be glad of the memories some day. They were right.

The blue elephant itself was in the box, along with the blanket and the other clothes we'd got from the women in the hospital. The contrast between the tiny body I remembered and the little dresses was ridiculous, even though they had been specially made for premature babies. I don't know how we ever thought they would fit. There was a tiny pink hat and two dresses, one in white, one a lemon colour. I was upset to read in the newspapers later that I had bought clothes in a toy shop for Jasmine. Even dolls' clothes would have been too big for her.

The nurses had remembered too to send me her hospital identity bracelet. This tag is normally around a patient's wrist, but Jasmine was so small that it had to go around her tummy. The box also contained a certificate from the chaplain at the hospital showing that Jasmine had been blessed and named on the morning of 19 May. This was another cop-out, I felt, as I had wanted my child to have a proper birth certificate instead of this piece of laminated paper. But legally she had never taken a breath and couldn't have a birth cert.

I kept the box with me at all times when I was in bed, no matter where I was sleeping. When I opened it up at night, the first thing I would take out was the identity bracelet. Because it had been around Jasmine's tummy and next to her skin, I felt I could get closer to her by touching it. There was a tiny drop of her blood on the elephant, and I would take that out next and inhale it, trying to smell her or get a sense of her. Of course, all I could smell was the scent of the hospital. Even so, I got some comfort from it.

I visited the cemetery every day. At times I thought I was losing my mind. I was still consumed by the fact that I had not had a chance to hold Jasmine or see her face. I became obsessed with wondering if her condition really had been as bad as I had been told it would be. I worried that I had done the wrong thing. The only way I would have known if she really had anencephaly, I thought, was if I had lifted up the blanket and looked at her properly. Now, it was too late to do that. Some evenings, standing by the side of the grave, I imagined digging her up and opening her coffin. I know it sounds insane, but I was desperate to see her, and the feeling overwhelmed me.

I walked up to the grave at all hours of the day or night, during all kinds of weather. Even though it got very dark at night, I had no fear of being there. Sometimes I would sit quietly beside the grave. At other times, I would stretch myself out on the soil, sobbing my heart out. There were times when I would kick at patches of clay, messing around with it, almost willing a hole to appear. I started to think I should just do it. I should dig her up. After all, she was my baby. Who was going to tell me I couldn't see my own baby? Even if I was arrested afterwards, it would be worth it because I would have been able to see my child.

I managed to talk sense to myself on those nights before doing anything stupid. I had become used to being my own counsellor and giving myself a good talking to when necessary. I told myself at those moments beside the grave that I needed to stop being dramatic and ridiculous. I made myself face the reality that I was never going to be able to see what I wanted to see. At best, if I had gone through with my desperate idea, I would have dug up bones. Gradually, over time, the impulse faded. But I still visited her regularly. Whenever I was sad or upset, when I rowed with my boyfriend or my mam, I would go and sit by Jasmine's grave and tell her about it.

It was a long time before we had money to fix the grave up properly. At first, it was surrounded by a white wooden fence. One day I came up to find most of the fence missing, and what remained was charred and broken. There was a wooden bench right beside the grave, and I could see beer cans and bottles strewn underneath it. The cemetery was sometimes used by young people who wanted somewhere quiet to drink, and they gravitated towards this seating area.

The family who owned the plot beside Jasmine's were tending their own grave when I discovered the damage. They didn't have much themselves, but one of the men, seeing how distraught I was, pressed €50 into my hand and insisted I take it to help replace the fencing.

I never got the headstone I wanted. My boyfriend's family were replacing a stone on their own family plot, and the old headstone was refurbished for Jasmine's grave. I wasn't consulted and had no say in the decision. Although I was grateful for the gesture, yet again I felt like she, and I, were afterthoughts.

The headstone was engraved with Jasmine's name and the date of her delivery, with two angels on either side. I was surprised the engraver had left so much blank space on the stone and asked my boyfriend's mother about it. She explained that it had been done in that way to leave enough room for my own name when I died, which made me feel very strange. As devastated as I was over what had happened, I had no intention of joining Jasmine any time soon. I tried to make the grave look as pretty as I could. I planted flowers and ensured it was always well-kept and colourful. I bought lots of ornaments and marble angels as presents for my little girl, to make up for her plain headstone.

My boyfriend and I tried to continue on as before, although I don't think our relationship was ever the same. What had happened shattered both of our lives, and we were each dealing with it in very different ways. The shock and grief had made him shut down emotionally, while I wanted to roar and shout and cry.

Circumstances pushed us closer than ever, however. In the eyes of the law, I was still a child, and someone was supposed to be responsible for me. We decided to get our own place to live. Under the law, I could become his legal dependent until I turned 18. He was only two years older than me; at 19 he was still only a young boy himself. Now he was under pressure to look after me and be my legal guardian. I felt as if I had become a burden to him, just as I was to everyone else.

Through a friend, we heard about a huge house in an estate on the other side of the river. It sounded fantastic. It was in a quiet, settled area and had five bedrooms. The landlord was a friend of someone we knew, so the rent was affordable. But it was also run-down and dirty.

This was an ideal project to occupy my mind. Along with my friend Danielle, I immediately tried to turn the filthy house into a home. The furniture in the house was torn and stained; the tiles were grubby and chipped. I spent a fortune on cleaning products and on pillows, cushions, candles and throws. We scrubbed, painted and cleaned it from top to bottom. All the effort I'd previously put into my appearance, I concentrated now on this house. I thought maybe I could still get that perfect family life I had imagined having with Jasmine.

To complete my little fantasy, I still longed for a baby. I had even told the journalist from the *Irish Independent* that I intended to be pregnant again within a year. As it turned out, it happened much more quickly than that.

Around six weeks after the funeral, a friend asked me to come up to the town centre with her. 'I think I'm pregnant,' she told me. We headed to the chemist and bought a double pack of pregnancy tests. She was too nervous to wait until we got home, so we went into the toilets in the nearby shopping centre. For fun, I decided I'd do a test too. Why not?

The toilets were packed. It was late afternoon and the secondary schools were finished for the day. My friend's test was negative. But the gang of schoolgirls doing their make-up at the sinks got a shock when they heard the noises coming from my cubicle. 'OH MY GOD! OH MY GOD!' I screamed, as the two lines appeared on my test.

I had wanted another baby so badly after what had happened to Jasmine. I had been using contraception but I hadn't been very careful about it. Now I was apprehensive about how my boyfriend would react. I wasn't sure if he felt the same way.

Things had continued to be very difficult between us since we'd returned from Liverpool. We had been together for so long, but the connection we once had was gone. We were two people living in the same house, and there was no bond between us any more. He had his friends round most nights and spent his evenings smoking and playing on his PlayStation with them. I had to cook and clean and felt like he wanted me to take his mammy's place.

When I told him about the pregnancy, he didn't believe me and thought I was winding him up. It was so soon after losing Jasmine. When he calmed down and realised I wasn't joking, he seemed to be happy, even though I could tell part of him wasn't too keen to go through all the drama again. We never felt like we were going to replace Jasmine. That's not what we were doing. This new baby would be their own little person.

We kept the news very close to home. We told our mothers and a few friends, but we didn't dare tell anyone else until around five months had passed. Both my mam and my boyfriend's mam were stunned when we first told them. Our families had just started to get over the trauma of the previous months. Now everyone was full of fear that something bad was going to happen again.

I was very well cared for, but every single day was a worry. I was on ten times the usual dose of folic acid, I took every pregnancy vitamin I could lay my hands on, and if a feather so much as brushed past my belly, I'd go into hospital to get checked out.

I was scanned very early in the pregnancy and got the best of care and attention in hospital. At each appointment, I braced myself for the confusion I expected to see in the eyes of the midwife, for the bad news they were going to tell me. But it never came. Every scan showed the baby growing just as it should have been, like a perfectly formed little coco pop. There were no signs of the terrible condition Jasmine had suffered from. I could see for myself that the baby's head looked normal – the images on the scans were totally different from what we had seen with her. Yet I had a hard time believing everything would be all right.

The big scan at 20 weeks pregnant was the one I was dreading most. Once again I lay down on the bed, and a friendly nurse squeezed the gel onto my tummy before taking out her probe. I closed my eyes, almost afraid to look at the screen or her face. But as the new baby's heartbeat echoed around the room, the nurse was smiling, reassuring me that everything still looked normal, as it had since the first scans they'd carried out. 'It's a boy!' she told us. 'A big, healthy baby boy.' After that, I began to relax a little. However, the sense of unease never fully left me for the whole pregnancy.

I was still attending Youthreach, occasionally. I enjoyed going there because it gave me a break from real life. While I was learning and studying, I remembered that I was still a young girl with a life ahead of me and a lot to learn. It gave me structure and a sense of normality. The teachers were supportive and made me feel safe.

Even though the court case and what had happened to me was not spoken about in class, the other students were aware I was the Miss D who had been in the newspapers and on the television. I knew I was being talked about behind my back. It was happening everywhere. I was standing in the queue to pay in Penneys one day when I saw a group of girls pointing at me. I could hear them whispering 'That's her, that's her'. It wasn't surprising, given how high-profile the case had been and how controversial the issue of abortion still was. But I struggled with becoming so well known in my hometown for what I felt were embarrassing and shameful reasons. I believed I was being judged everywhere I went.

I also suspected some of the people I considered to be friends were talking to the media. At the end of the court case, a damning photograph of me had appeared in one of the tabloids. Even though my face was pixelated, to me it was obviously recognisable. I was wearing a short red dress and holding a bottle of Smirnoff Ice in one hand and a cigarette in the other. The photograph had been taken back in 2005, but that wasn't clear from the article. The implication was that I had been drinking and smoking during my pregnancy with Jasmine and that it had contributed to what had happened to her. The photograph devastated me, and it upset me even more to think that it must have come from someone I knew.

All these weeks after the court case, I was also still getting phone calls from newspapers. Sometimes reporters would call to my door, wanting to know if I was pregnant again. One newspaper offered me money – €300! – for me to tell them where my child's grave was so they could get a picture. Some of them told me that if I didn't speak to them they'd find someone else who would give them information about me. I suppose it's no wonder that I became paranoid.

Once my new pregnancy became obvious, I became self-conscious about going into Youthreach every day. I couldn't deny what was happening, but I didn't want to talk about it, and I was tired of being gossiped about. My teachers tried to persuade me not to leave. They knew I was smart. And they worried, rightly, about what would happen to me and my baby if I didn't have any kind of qualification. My boyfriend, on the other hand, didn't try to change my mind about dropping out. He had never liked me doing the course. When I came home, he used to quiz me about who I had seen and what I had done. He checked what I was wearing every day and told me friends of his were keeping an eye on me. It bugged me a little bit, but most of the time I saw this behaviour as an example of how much he cared about me and wanted to protect me.

Leaving Youthreach meant I was back to being almost completely dependent on my boyfriend. We argued constantly, and the fights got worse as my pregnancy progressed. I couldn't tell anyone what was going on between us. My mam was still not able to be emotionally there for me. His mother had her other children to deal with and didn't really want to know. I was also afraid to say too much to his family, because I didn't want to ruin my relationship with them.

The first contractions came just two weeks before my 18th birthday, less than a year since I had given birth to Jasmine. The pains, even though they were mild at first, immediately brought back the worst memories. As they intensified, I began to lose my grip on reality.

The labour went on for hours. At its peak, I became hysterical. I stopped pushing and started screaming as the midwives tried to calm me down. It was no good. In my head I was back in Liverpool Women's Hospital and this wasn't my son coming out: I was reliving Jasmine's birth. I became terrified by what this new baby would look like. I told the midwives that I couldn't do it, I wouldn't do it, I was not having this baby.

My extreme reaction was almost certainly some of the stress and shock surrounding Jasmine's birth finally being released. It probably would have taken years of therapy to deal with the trauma I was going through and to process my fears properly. But there was no time for therapy in the labour ward at Our Lady of Lourdes Hospital in Drogheda. This baby wasn't going to wait around. He was coming out no matter how much I protested. As he was born, I asked the nurses if he was alive. So many bad things had happened to me and I was always expecting the worst.

To my shock, my new baby boy was absolutely perfect. We named him Adam, and he was healthy and beautiful.

There seemed to be far too many people in the delivery room as I was giving birth: my boyfriend, our mothers, even my older sister Sharon was there, encouraging me as I pushed. Everyone wanted to see him. We were all overcome with relief and joy. Neither family had a grandchild, and everyone was immediately obsessed with him. I was surrounded by a huge bubble of love, and I could pretend to myself that this love was meant for me as much as it was for Adam.

When the visitors finally left, I looked at my son. He was dark eyed with a full head of dark hair, just like me and my father. Looking at him that first night, I made some decisions. I decided we were not going to be poor. We were not going to be homeless. We were going to be safe, and happy. I wanted a new future with Adam, and I made him a promise: I was not going to let the bad world get in on him the way it had got in on me.

8

NEW BEGINNINGS

My son was a beautiful diamond, my saving grace. He saved my mother too. By the time he was a month old, I had made up my mind: I was determined to change my life and give him everything he deserved.

Some things had already changed for the better. I had moved to a lovely, modern three-bedroom house in an estate I had lived in before with my mother. I worked out that I had lived in around 15 separate places since our arrival in Drogheda six years previously, including foster homes and bed and breakfast accommodation. This was my chance to have a bit of stability at last and to make a new home for myself and for my son.

Adam was thriving. He was a gorgeous, chubby, happy baby, doted on by everyone. I wanted him to have a good life, and I knew this meant I had to get my own life in order. I wanted a job – not just a job, a career. I wanted to finally finish school, and I wanted to go to college.

Miss D was still following me around, however. Adam's birth brought the newspaper reporters back into my life. Everyone wanted a story about Miss D's new baby on the first anniversary of the controversial court case. When he was only a few weeks old, a reporter and a photographer called to the house, catching me by surprise. We chatted, and they asked if the photographer could take Adam's picture. I thought they were offering to take it purely for my benefit. I mean, he was such a gorgeous, button-eyed little baby – why wouldn't they want to take a photo? I also knew they couldn't identify me, so I was confident they couldn't make a photograph of my baby public.

I was stunned the next morning when my mam rang me and told me to get a copy of the newspaper. They had used the photograph after all, in an article about 'Miss D's new baby'. In a bizarre attempt to stick to the rules and disguise Adam's identity, they had put a black bar across his face. It wasn't even across his eyes. It was like a strange blip across his nose and mouth. I was appalled, and the photograph caused me no end of trouble in my community. People presumed I had sold a picture of my baby to the media. My boyfriend and his family knew I had been paid for the interview I did after the court case, and they assumed I got money for this too. I don't think they ever believed my denials.

I turned 18 just two weeks after Adam's birth, and as an adult, I was no longer the HSE's problem. They needed to make sure Adam was all right, though, and I was assigned a social worker to check in on me and help me with my parenting skills. Ciara was shaven-headed, kind and caring. She became more of a friend to me than a social worker. I didn't feel like just another one of her cases. She helped me in the difficult early days of parenting, and she listened as I told her about my hopes and dreams for the future. She strongly encouraged me to get back into education.

That September, supported by Ciara, I went back to school. I began attending a course called Building Your Future, specifically for young mothers who had left school early. I was the baby of the group. There were many women in their late twenties who had had kids and wanted to get back into work. We did subjects like English, computers, manual handling, fire safety, first aid – anything that could get us into college or into a job.

My boyfriend was not supportive. He wasn't interested in going to college, and he couldn't understand why I was. He had no interest in discussing my course or my hopes for the future and it was hard to get the backup I needed to mind Adam.

I also felt horribly unattractive. Even though I was only 18, I felt much older. Two back-to-back pregnancies had destroyed my body. I hated the stretch marks all over my stomach and hips. These 'tiger stripes', as I called them, were so noticeable that sometimes my boyfriend would encourage me to show them to his mates when they called round, just for a laugh.

I bonded with the women on my course, who could tell things weren't good at home, even if they didn't know the details. The course leader, Linda, was one of the most supportive people I could have wished to have in my life. She helped me with my education, but also checked in to make sure I was OK emotionally. She gave me guidance, encouraged me to have a goal and spurred me on to be excited about the future.

Back then, maths came easily to me, and Linda encouraged me to take the higher-level option. Our coursework and our assignments during the year of the course all went towards our final Leaving Certificate marks. When Linda handed me the envelope containing my results, she had a big grin. I opened them, and I was left speechless, for once. I had passed with distinction! I was shocked and delighted. This was proof to me that I was on the right track – despite everything, there was still a way for me to better myself and to achieve my dreams. It was a big deal to me because it meant I could now go to college.

Linda encouraged me to apply for a course at Drogheda Institute of Further Education. If you had really pushed me about what my dream course would have been, I would have said acting. I grew up wanting to be an actor and was often told, not always in a complimentary way, that I was a very dramatic person. In school, I had also thought of being a chef. My dream would probably have been to be a chef on the telly! But I had to be realistic. I had to choose a course in Drogheda, where I could be close to my home and I had options for minding my baby, so I picked beauty therapy. It seemed fun and exciting and fitted in perfectly with my love of costume, make-up and dressing up.

Adam was more than a year old now. My mother was starting to play a much bigger part in our lives. She knew she had to stay healthy to rebuild her relationship with her family. Gradually, I had begun to realise that she was someone I could depend on again, and she would often mind Adam for me while I studied. She was also aware that my home life was becoming unbearable and that I needed her. She had a new sense of worth and of purpose.

The situation with my boyfriend came to a head one afternoon, near his mother's house. I had gone down with Adam to ask him to come home and mind the baby for a while. He refused, and there was a nasty argument in the street, with around a dozen people watching. He told me he needed a break and was going to stay with his mother for a while. I went home and decided I was not going to let my child witness any more of these rows.

After six weeks of being looked after by his mammy, my boyfriend decided he wanted to come back. I had been processing our break-up, however. I had grown stronger and had begun to believe in myself and my ability to get by without him. My chats with the other women on my course had helped me get clarity about how I should be treated.

I had thought a lot about my future. I knew it would be hard on my own, but I knew I could do it. As a child, I had worshipped my mam, and even after everything that had happened, I still adored her. I focused on the unconditional love between a parent and child. I could help Adam grow and flourish and that excited me. When things went wrong for my mam, she had become less of a mother to me. I wanted to make sure that didn't happen to me and Adam. What had been good enough for me to put up with in the relationship was not going to be good enough for my child. I told my boyfriend I didn't want him back.

Separating from him was difficult. I still find it hard to be a single mother. And we had been through so much together. He was my first real love, or at least the first person I thought I was in love with. I didn't understand what love really was and hadn't seen many healthy relationships among the adults in my life to model my own on. We were both damaged people and had clung to each other fiercely.

Jasmine's condition and the craziness of the court case

had forced us together in a very stressful environment. It hadn't been easy for either for us since the day of Jasmine's diagnosis. We'd been through two pregnancies. I had been either pregnant or suffering from the after-effects of what had happened with Jasmine for two years. He had dealt with the pain in his own way. It just wasn't working any more. My horizons were widening and I wanted to move on, to create a better life for our family. He didn't seem to be interested in moving on with me.

So now I was on my own and more determined than ever to make the most of any opportunity I was given.

Everywhere I had been previously, it seemed people knew almost everything about me. They knew my boyfriend or they knew about my mam or they knew about my baby. College was an opportunity to rebrand myself. In college, no one knew anything. They didn't know I was Miss D. I wasn't notorious for going out with the local 'bad boy'. All of a sudden, at 20 years of age, I had the chance to live the life of a normal young person – with college and parties and nights out.

I tried to live that life, even though I was the only young mother in the class. I played down the fact that I had a child. I wasn't exactly trying to hide it, but I didn't like to talk about it too much. I felt embarrassed and ashamed that I was a single mother at such a young age. I still felt there was a stigma attached to it. I was slightly older than a lot of the girls who were straight out of school, and much younger than the mature students in their thirties and forties. The younger girls were in their late teens, living at home with their parents, and I tried not to draw attention to how different my life was from theirs.

I was working in a clothes shop, supporting myself through the course and paying for Adam to be in crèche. In my first year, I didn't spend a lot of money on myself. My money all went on getting through college, and whatever spare time I had went on Adam. At times, I stuck my head in the sand and didn't want to open the bills that came through the door, although I managed to make it work most of time. I had a lot on my plate, and sometimes during that first year, I wondered why I was bothering and thought seriously about giving it all up.

Sue, my tutor, spotted that I was struggling. She pulled me aside one day and gave me a good talking to about why I wasn't keeping up with my work. I was full of excuses about how difficult it was for me. She told me in no uncertain terms that being a mother, even a single mother, was no excuse at all. She taught me to get my books out no matter where I was. Even while cooking dinner, or feeding Adam, she told me, I should have my books open on the kitchen counter. I learned how to juggle, and I got through the work with her help. Without Sue's advice, I wouldn't have finished that first year. When I passed my end of year exams, I was so grateful to her and so proud of myself. I was another step closer to making a new life.

Although things were looking up for me academically, I was still insecure about my appearance. It was at a time when the internet and smartphones were becoming more prevalent and images of what a woman 'should' look like were everywhere. Towards the end of my relationship with my boyfriend, he had developed a growing interest in pornography. It seemed so easy to get access to the stuff he wanted to watch, and all his friends seemed to watch it too. I felt I was in competition with this new world. I looked at the kind of women he was giving his attention to, and I felt that I just couldn't win with my stretch-marked, post-baby body.

I had lost all my confidence. I was too embarrassed to wear bikinis, and I avoided going swimming. At college, we beauty students would bump into the lads who were studying the sports courses. Some of the other girls would tell the boys that I had a child, and no one would ever come near me. I was rarely asked out on dates, and I probably would have been too self-conscious to go.

I know it's awful that I felt so bad about how I looked. I'm fully aware I was comparing my appearance to what media images were promoting and my idea of what people like my ex-boyfriend thought was attractive. But I couldn't help it. I was miserable and I knew I needed to do something about it. I felt like a beaten down, tired, saggy person who had become old before her time.

It was a customer in a bar I was working in who suggested a solution for my stretch marks. Dualta owned a tattoo parlour and, one night when we sat talking, he told me he could help me.

I already had one tattoo on my right hip, which I got before I became pregnant with Jasmine. It was an image of a rose on a stem with a heart, and I had told myself it was in honour of my mother, whose name is Rosaleen. If I'm honest, it wasn't just about my mother – really, I was looking for any excuse to get a tattoo. But at the time I was also worried about my mam and concerned she was going to die. Her life was in danger so many times because of the way she was living. We always thought we might lose her in a few months or a year at most. I lived like that for a long time.

Like the rest of my body, the rose had been ravaged by my pregnancies. But Dualta took inspiration from it and began a pattern of roses across my stomach. I got two tattoos specifically to honour Jasmine. The first was a drawing of a Day of the Dead 'princess', as I knew her, or La Catrina – a symbol of the Mexican celebration of the Day of the Dead. I had become fascinated by how the Mexicans treated death and their traditions of protecting and honouring those who had passed away. My lady of the dead had an earring in the shape of the letter J in memory of my daughter, but without being too obvious to anyone who would see it. I loved the tattoos and they covered up all the marks I was so embarrassed about. I felt young again.

I also joined a gym and began working out daily, sometimes twice a day. The trainers thought I had potential and were working really hard with me. My confidence started to come back. I regained my love of clothes. I started dressing better, feeling better and attracting more attention. I also managed to pass my exams while I was at it. By the middle of 2011, I was a fully qualified beauty therapist and masseuse.

My tattoo artist friend, Dualta, had told me I should think about getting into modelling. I didn't take him too seriously. He wasn't the first person to have suggested this to me. But I was short and I was never a size zero, so it was always something I dismissed and put to the back of my mind. In 2010 and 2011, as my confidence grew, I started doing some promotional work for local businesses. I signed up to the Assets Modelling Agency as a commercial model and became the 'face' of my gym.

In early 2012 I spotted an ad in the *Star* newspaper looking to find the 'Babe of the Year'. I sent in an entry, thinking I would hear nothing back. To my surprise, they rang me and, out of thousands of entries, I became one of the 12 finalists.

Our pictures appeared in the newspaper. But the highlight of the whole event was a motorbike show in the RDS exhibition centre in Dublin in March that year. The other girls and I were dressed up in our 'babe' outfits – bright-pink one-piece leotards with check collars and tiny check skirts. We wore sky-high heels, climbed onto Harley Davidsons and garda motorbikes and strutted around the exhibition all day. Our job was to pose for photos with anyone who wanted one and to walk on stage every hour. There were bikers and motorbikes everywhere, as well as firebreathers and acrobats.

These kinds of competitions try to sell themselves as being all about empowerment and building women up, but the reality is very different. If you asked me about entering such a competition now, I'd tell you how disgraceful it is that women are pitted against each other. I'd say that these beauty competitions don't build up confidence – instead, they knock women down. They send out a message that if you don't look like a 'babe', you're nothing. They're not about career or drive or ambition: they're about boobs and bums and how willing you are to wear very little. We thought we were in control, but really we had no control over what we wore or how we were portrayed.

I did not think like that at the time, however. Back then, I loved my first taste of this new world. I thought I was going to have a career in modelling. This was going to be my life. I was going to meet a rich man and I could already see myself moving to Beverly Hills!

The motorbike show lasted the whole weekend. Photographers followed us around every day and gazed up at us on stage, looking for their shot. Some approached us and offered us the chance to do shoots for our portfolios. This was before Instagram, where everyone can now carefully curate their own image and girls have a bit more control. These photographers talked about modelling, and more specifically glamour modelling – I didn't really know there was a difference. I just heard the word 'modelling' and there were stars in my eyes.

I did several 'glamour' shoots after the show. The photographers would reassure me that, even though I was posing naked, no one would be able to see anything compromising in the final shots. There would be strategically placed blankets, or leaves or other props. But, of course, the photographers themselves got to see everything. At the time I was happy with the final results. But I regretted it afterwards and later began to warn other young girls against doing such shoots.

One of the reasons I got into modelling was to get as far away as possible from Miss D. I was trying to wipe out the shame of the court case and of being known for travelling to England for an abortion. I was overcompensating in an effort to give people a totally different reason to know my name. But once I had signed the copyright away on my photographs, I had no control over where the images would end up. Some are still on the internet. Sometimes the glamour shots ended up in articles about Miss D. It frustrated me deeply when those two worlds collided.

The Babe of the Year show led to other competitions, many of them organised by a company called Diva Next Door. I made the finals of some of the shows. I never won, but it wasn't about winning for me. I was just delighted to be involved in these events, which were so far away from the kind of life I had been living. As a finalist in the competition one year, I ended up at a beautiful ball in a hotel in Ballsbridge in Dublin, wearing a gorgeous gown, with some of the top models in Ireland as the judges.

With my height and body type, I was never asked to do high-fashion shoots, but I was in demand for lingerie and swimwear. Once I had done one or two such shoots, people came looking for me to do more, and it became normal for me. All the other girls in the competitions did them too. It was totally accepted. Among the other girls, I would probably have been seen as quite timid or conservative. Back home in Drogheda, I was considered crazy – someone who had tickets on herself and was doing all these sexy shoots and competitions down in Dublin.

I modelled in fashion shows for people starting their own clothing lines; I wore bridal dresses and ball gowns. I was asked to attend birthday parties for wealthy people where my only job was to stand around looking glamorous. I was paid to have make-up applied to my face. I worked in nightclubs as a hostess. I attended events where all I had to do was hold trays of food or drink and look pretty. I also dressed up in ridiculous costumes to promote everything from drinks to sandwich bars. I could be a character from Game of Thrones one day and a bunny rabbit the next.

I was even a contender to be the Louth Rose for the Rose of Tralee competition. Some of the organisers asked me to apply after seeing my picture in the newspaper. At that time, because of my experience in Dublin, I was the go-to girl in Drogheda if anyone wanted to promote anything, so I was frequently pictured in the local paper.

I really did not fit in with the other potential Roses. Again, I was the only young mother in the group, and I was also a lot more outspoken than many of them. They were a really nice group of women, though, and there was much less bitchiness among them than in some of the competitions I'd been involved in in Dublin. I got to wear beautiful clothes and take part in lots of events, although I did not become the Louth Rose!

I spent my early twenties in the VIP areas of various Dublin nightclubs. I often brought my sister Sharon with me, and one night we were invited into the VIP section of a venue in North Dublin with 50 Cent and other rappers who had just finished a gig in the city centre. They told us we had a choice – we could take some photos and leave, or we could put our phones away and enjoy ourselves. We handed in our phones to a security guard and drank Patrón tequila with them until the early hours. On nights like that, the events of 2007 were very far from my mind.

Mam helped me a lot by minding Adam in the evenings and at weekends so that I could take part in all of this. Every bit of the good life I was beginning to enjoy was because of her support. I think she understood my desire to put myself out there and get away from my past. I didn't ask for her opinion or her permission, however. No one was allowed to have an opinion on the modelling. I was doing it no matter what anyone else thought of it. It's one part of my life I am not completely ashamed of. I look back at my innocence and my hope that I was going to become a star, and I sometimes think what a poor deluded eejit I was! But it was still a good time in my life, a whirlwind of parties, clubs and photo shoots.

One of the drawbacks about putting yourself out there at that time was that it wasn't cool to be nice. Everyone now talks about 'being kind', even if they don't always practise what they preach. Back then, people could be quite rude to each other and almost revelled in putting one another down. Because I was one of the only mothers doing that kind of work, it gave me a different perspective on it all. It wasn't the most important thing in my life.

When people asked me how many children I had, I was always confused about what I should answer. How could I explain? I didn't feel I could tell them about the first pregnancy and everything that happened around it. It's a lot to bring into an everyday conversation and far too much to expect people to understand. If I mentioned Jasmine, I felt I had to explain everything – her condition, the court case, how I gave birth to her. I usually avoided it and just talked about Adam.

I felt guilty about ignoring her though. And I wanted to do something more to remember her, something that would be a constant reminder that she was always with me. When Adam was around seven years old, my boyfriend at the time was another tattoo artist, and I often spent evenings drinking coffee and chatting with him in his studio. I remembered the laminated card I had been given by the Liverpool hospital with Jasmine's tiny footprints on it. My boyfriend came up with a design incorporating her little feet as well as a daisy with a fallen petal, which we decided to put on the inside of my left wrist. The feet are an exact copy of her footprints and exactly the same size.

I've never regretted my tattoos, and especially not that one. It was a recognition of Jasmine, and for me it meant her existence could not be denied. It was my way of remembering that I had two children. Of course, Jasmine means a lot more to me than just a tattoo, but it shows she is not forgotten. She may not have had a birth certificate, but her little footprints on my wrist remind me every day that she was 'real'.

Sadly, the relationship with the tattoo artist ended, and even though I dated other people from time to time, I spent a lot of time on my own. In late 2017, my best friends decided they were going to take matters into their own hands. One of my friends, Dani, was getting married. The others were all in relationships. I was the only singleton in the group. My friends saw an ad for a new dating series on RTÉ. *First Dates Ireland* was a version of a UK series where producers set couples up on blind dates and then filmed their interactions.

Dani filmed my audition video in my living room and sent in the application for me. She was just doing it for a bit of fun, and we jumped around my kitchen when we got news that I had been chosen to be on the show. I secretly hoped it might lead to something more serious. Part of me foolishly hoped I might actually find love.

Mam and I were now inseparable, and she came with me to the hotel where the programme was being shot. It was a lunchtime date, which was nerve-wracking. I was the main 'dater' in that episode, and the producers treated me like a princess. I had been asked to describe in detail the kind of man I would like to meet, so I was hopeful that he might at least be handsome and tall. But my date had none of the characteristics I had suggested, except that he was male.

I was sitting on a stool waiting for my date to walk in when I saw a guy I recognised. His name was Phil, and he had been one of the 'stars' of a short-lived reality television programme called Tallafornia a few years previously. My heart immediately sank. He didn't have a good reputation on the show, particularly when it came to women. Our date showed he hadn't changed.

He was astonishingly rude to me. He told me I had 'a nice little hoop'. He asked me if my breasts were real and if I'd had my lips done. He made me pay for half the meal and tried to kiss me. I can only assume the producers saw my dramatic, expressive personality and his controversial attitude and thought, 'Together, they would make good television.'

He was unbelievably derogatory towards me, and I felt horrible. Halfway through the date I excused myself and went to have a little cry in the toilets. At the time I was working as a supervisor in an upmarket clothes shop. I was used to getting dressed up every day and presenting myself well, and this guy was treating me like a piece of trash. However, I forced myself back to the table and continued the 'date'. Our appearance and his terrible attitude generated newspaper headlines for days afterwards, and we appeared on a national radio show where he half-heartedly apologised to me.

I knew I was being used to create controversy and generate headlines. Despite that, strange as it seems, I was glad I did the show. I felt people really got to see the real me. And best of all, Miss D was never mentioned, even though the producers knew about my past. But at the same time, Phil's attitude towards me unnerved me. I wondered what it was about my appearance that made him think he could talk to me like that. Yes, I made an effort to look glamorous. Did that mean I didn't deserve respect? As usual, I began to find fault with myself. I wondered, not for the first time, if I was to blame for the way men treated me.

9

ESCAPING THE PAST

first met Eamonn outside my mother's house in around 2014. I was just heading home, and Mam and I were standing in the garden chatting when he pulled up in his van.

Eamonn Byrne was in his fifties, around the same age as Mam, grey-haired and slightly dishevelled looking. He delivered groceries in the area and sometimes stopped to talk to my mother. He greeted me warmly. 'Hello, love!' The two young lads who worked with him were grinning and waving at me – I'd been in school with both of them.

He hopped out of the van and Mam introduced him to me. After that, I saw him quite regularly at my mother's place and we'd always talk. He offered to deliver shopping to my own house. I refused – I didn't want to buy what he was selling. I was 24 years old, I had one child, and I didn't need industrial-sized boxes of washing powder or crates of Coca-Cola.

Despite this, he started calling to my house anyway. The boys would usually be with him, and we'd all have a bit of a chat and a laugh at the door. Once or twice I bought a crate of Coke or a box of detergent, just to be kind. On other occasions he'd insist on me taking vegetables or other groceries, even when I didn't want them.

He often called on Saturday mornings, when there was time to talk. It was nice to have someone to chat to, someone who seemed to care. He rapidly became a grandfatherly or father figure to me. I was always looking for someone to replace the dad I didn't have.

I'm an open book and find it hard to disguise my emotions. When Eamonn called, he could immediately see from my face whether I was having a good or a bad week, and after a little bit of prodding, I would tell him everything that was going on in my life. He knew about my childhood, about my relationship issues, about my background and the Miss D court case. Some of this he knew before I ever told him. I didn't feel uncomfortable or uneasy with him. He frequently called when my boyfriend at the time was around, when I was with my son, or when my mother was there, and he would almost always have the lads with him. I never felt anything strange or untoward was going on.

My then partner, however, started to get a bit annoyed by how regularly Eamonn appeared. He had given me a box for my television and called from time to time to check on the box and update it. Sometimes he appeared to be a little drunk. I felt sorry for him on these occasions, and I would still chat to him at the door.

He would often call me just when I was heading out. I didn't have a car at the time, and I usually walked the short distance to collect my son from school. Eamonn lived in the area. He would appear on the road in his van and offer to bring me to collect Adam and then drop us home. I didn't think there was anything wrong with this. I saw him as someone who cared about me and just happened to be thinking of me as he passed by my estate. He had become part of the family.

My mam and my boyfriend, on the other hand, started to get a little worried. At one stage, Eamonn even suggested that my son and I should join him on a holiday to Spain, saying friends of his were no longer able to go. Thankfully, I didn't accept that invitation.

In mid-2016, my boyfriend and I broke up, and Eamonn's visits became more regular still. I was upset about the break-up and confided in him. He was caring and kind and easy to talk to.

At around this time, items started turning up at the door of my home. If I was out with my friends at night, I sometimes came home to find a bag of freshly picked apples on the doorstep or a bag of my favourite Haribo sweets. It wasn't cute or nice, even though it may have been intended that way. It was scary knowing that someone had been creeping around outside my house late at night, leaving things at my front door. It never crossed my mind that Eamon might have been the one responsible. Then, the text messages started.

The messages came from numbers I didn't know. The sender was able to tell me exactly where I was and when. They knew when I was at home and when I was at work. The messages asked me what kind of underwear I was wearing, or they said they'd seen me behind the bar of the pub I worked in at the time and commented on how sexy I looked. There were dozens of messages, always sent at night, from different numbers. At the start, I thought it was someone trying to annoy me and that they had just made lucky guesses about what I was wearing or where I was. But as the messages kept coming, I began to get scared.

I told Eamonn what was happening, and he seemed very concerned. He was calling to my house a little too often at that time. Sometimes I asked my mam to tell him to go away, or I would try to ignore the doorbell. I still didn't suspect that he meant me any harm. I was just beginning to feel he was around my life far too much and I had enough to be dealing with.

One Thursday I came back late from an evening out with my friends. My usual schedule meant that my son used to stay with his dad on Thursdays, something anyone who knew me would have known. When I opened my front door, I was hit by a breeze blowing through the house and found a back window had been jammed open. Panicking, I ran out of the house and sprinted up the road to find a friend to come back in with me. Sure enough, my house had been broken into, but it was a very unusual break-in.

What was strange was that nothing of value seemed to have been taken. Jewellery, money I had left out, Adam's iPad and his PlayStation – they were all still there. My bedroom, however, had been destroyed. Drawers and wardrobes had been thrown open. My make-up and my underwear were strewn around the room.

I was in shock and terrified. The guards came and took statements, and I called my mam, who brought me to the local pub to try to calm me down. While we were there, my phone rang. It was Eamonn. 'Hi,' he said, concern in his voice, 'I've just heard you've been broken into. Would you like me to come down and stay with you, to keep you company?' It was only an hour or so since I'd discovered the break-in. He told me I didn't need to bother with the Gardaí – that they weren't going to be able to do anything for me. That was the final straw as far as my mother was concerned: she grabbed the phone from me, ordered him to stay away from her daughter and told me never to let him near the house again.

Although the people around me were now highly

suspicious of Eamonn's motives, it still didn't occur to me that he could have anything to do with the vile text messages I was receiving. I had only reported the text messages to the Gardaí after the break-in, in case there was a connection. One Saturday morning in late 2016, two gardaí called to my door. They asked me to sit down before explaining that they had discovered who had been sending the texts. When they said it was Eamonn, I refused to believe them. He cared about me! Our relationship had become a bit dysfunctional in the previous months, but it couldn't be him, surely.

The Gardaí outlined the case they had been building. They had proof that he had been buying SIM cards in Tesco and phone credit from a UK mobile phone company in order to send the messages from different numbers. I had a sick, hollow feeling in the pit of my stomach. It was as if I had been completely violated. My trust had been utterly betrayed.

I discovered that Eamonn had been trying to contact me over social media in the years before I had ever met him at my mother's house. When I was modelling, I received lots of explicit messages on my Facebook pages. I dealt with them by ignoring most of them or setting up new pages. But when I looked back at old pictures, I saw comments from Eamonn on some of them, telling me how sexy I was. I thought he saw me as a daughter and wanted to protect me. It disturbed me that he saw me in a sexual way, and now it seemed he had been willing to torture me with horrible text messages.

I blamed myself as usual. What had I done to cause this? How had I not noticed? I thought he was caring for me, and I also thought I was being kind to him. I believed that, like me, he was a little lonely and needed someone to talk to. I felt embarrassed, naïve and stupid. I felt I had a problem with men, that I didn't trust the right people, and that I was willing to be comforted by anyone who showed me the slightest bit of compassion. I had put myself in this position.

Eamonn was charged with harassing and stalking me. But the case took a long time to get to court, and the ordeal went on much longer than I had anticipated. Months passed by, then years. He lived nearby and I often saw him in the local shop. It was torture. I had lost all sense of security. Every time I came back to the house after being out, I would ring my mother or a friend and would not allow them to get off the line until I had checked all the doors and windows, all the rooms and all the wardrobes to make sure my home was safe.

A date was finally set for a hearing of the case in the district court in Drogheda towards the end of September 2020 – four years after I had first reported the text messages. I was looking forward to it coming to an end. I knew that Eamonn intended to plead guilty to harassing me between August and November 2016, and I had been asked to prepare a victim impact statement. I felt constrained by the rules around preparing such statements, and I didn't feel I fully expressed the mental trauma I had experienced as a result of his actions. Nevertheless, I became emotional as read it out in the packed courtroom. I told the court I had lost trust and confidence as a result of what had happened.

I was shaking as I returned to my seat after giving my statement. Unlike my experience in court in 2007, this time I had been given a voice, even if I didn't get to say everything I wanted. Eamonn was staring at me the whole time I was in the courtroom. Everyone could see it, but no one could do anything about it. 'He won't be able to stare at me from his prison cell,' I thought.

He got into the witness box next and finally apologised to me. He said he understood the effect his actions had on me and that it would never happen again. It meant little to me. I didn't believe him and wanted to see him punished. I thought I would get justice.

The judge – a woman – seemed to take the crimes seriously. She described what had happened as 'absolutely despicable'. And she said she was concerned by some of what Eamonn had said to probation officers. He had told them he didn't frighten me because I was someone who 'wasn't easily frightened'. It was as if he was suggesting that because I had been through so much, I shouldn't have been scared by some text messages. The judge pointed out that I had confided in him, and she criticised his attempts to justify what he had done.

The judge said she was 'not impressed' and imposed a four-month prison sentence, but her next words knocked the wind out of me. She suspended the sentence entirely, mainly because it had taken so long for the case to get to court. Eamonn was ordered to stay away from me for a year, but he was free to go.

That was it. It was over. The case that had been hanging over me for four years ended, with no justice as far as I was concerned. We all walked out of court. I was bawling crying. The investigating guards didn't know what to say to me. I was convinced Eamonn was almost smirking. I had been through so much stress to get to this point, all for nothing.

We stood around, shocked, in the grounds of the large courthouse where the case had been heard. Eamonn was standing near me – too near. I was livid. Adrenalin took over and I lost my temper. In front of the crowds of gardaí, lawyers, prison officers and security guards, I threw the remains of my cold cup of coffee over him and started trying to hit him. Mam was a few feet away and rushed over to help me. I thought I would be taken away in handcuffs, but no one stopped me. Still sobbing, I left the court precinct and drove home with my mam.

The newspapers reported on the case the next day, and one journalist interviewed me for my reaction. By this stage, I had discovered that, under the law, a sentence imposed by the district court could not be appealed by the Director of Public Prosecutions for being too lenient. Prosecuting authorities could appeal sentences in higher courts but not in this one. It was an oversight, and there had been discussions for many years about changing the law, but nothing had happened, and now it would be too late for me.

The comments started shortly after the newspaper articles appeared. I heard from my mother that people were saying I'd sold my story and that I was making money from the newspapers off the back of it. It brought me back to 2007 and the remarks made about me then.

I felt suffocated again. Nothing could be done about the sentence. I had to let it go. I had waited years to get justice for what this man had done, and he got a slap on the wrist. I had done everything right – I had reported it; I had asked the guards to deal with it.

I felt I had been repeatedly let down, every single time I tried to do the right thing. My life had become a circus in the High Court just because I had tried to do what was right. Now I had been stalked and broken into, and I hadn't got what I needed from the legal system. No one was ever charged with the break-in.

I was beginning to feel something was really wrong with me. Why did things like this keep happening to me, and only to me? What was I doing wrong? I'd never heard of anyone else being in the kinds of situations I had found myself in over the years. People were telling me I was too nice, too trusting. I thought I should have done more to avoid these situations. Was I too dramatic? Was there something about me that made me vulnerable? Was there something that men could see in me and take advantage of?

I had believed for many years that one of the reasons I had so many problems in my life was my lack of a father. When my father left Ireland after his first visit to my mam and me, his relationship with us fizzled out. My mam never had a good word to say about him. I thought she was being bitter and horrible, but of course now I can see that he didn't do anything for either of us and she had to raise me on her own. He had lied to her about everything – his use of drugs, his health and even his age. He was seven years older than my mam, but he hadn't admitted that to her when she first met him and had pretended he was in his twenties like her.

All through my childhood years, I really wished I had a dad. I liked telling people about him and loved just being able to say the word 'dad'. I had an extremely romantic view of him. I told friends that he was in San Francisco playing in a rock band. I had almost convinced myself that was the reason we never saw him. Obviously, he was just too busy on tour.

My longing for a father grew as I became a teenager and my relationship with my mother began to deteriorate. It was then my mother told me about finding out he was on methadone when he came to visit us. When I was born, in 1990, the stigma attached to being a heroin addict was even worse than it is now. It was something my mother just wouldn't tolerate.

As life became more difficult, I had a recurring fantasy that my dad would come and save me. I tracked down contact details for him through his brother's business, and I wrote to him every so often. We exchanged a few emails and letters over the years, but it was very sporadic. I would get two letters from him in one year and then nothing for a couple of years. His letters, when they did come, often included poetry and song lyrics he had written for me, fuelling my romanticised view of him as a tortured rock star.

In my imagination, I still believed lots of my problems would have been solved if I had a strong father by my side. When my mam was struggling, I had no one to rescue me. I thought if my dad had been around, he would never have let the HSE stop me from going to England. My dad would have ensured I was treated properly. He might never have let me get involved with my boyfriend in the first place, and he would certainly have taken him on when our relationship went bad. All throughout the worst years, I had this vision that he would one day just turn up at the front door and sort everything out.

I wrote to him when the court case was going on and after I had Adam, letter after letter, setting out what had happened and cheerily assuring him everything had turned out all right. I still have those letters today, with their heartbreaking requests for him to contact me. I never sent them. I was afraid he would think I wanted something from him. I was too proud to tell him the truth and worried he would get scared off and end the little contact we had. I imagined conversations in which I would tell him everything and he would make it all right. But on the few occasions I did actually speak to him on the phone, I didn't tell him any details of the trauma I was going through. I didn't want him to think I was a victim, and I was afraid of being rejected.

I moved so many times and life became so chaotic that we lost touch completely. But in 2018, I came up with a plan. If he wouldn't or couldn't come to see me, I would go and visit him in the United States. I wanted to be able to say that I had met my dad, that I wasn't fatherless. My mam was a dramatic, quirky character. However, I believed a lot of my own dramatic expressiveness must have come from dad and his Italian heritage. I knew I had his nose and his dark, frizzy, curly hair. I wanted to see him in person.

I was annoyed that he wasn't making the effort to have

contact with me. Nevertheless, I tracked down his details, again, and made my plans. Through his family members, I learned he had problems with his heart and hadn't been well in the years since he'd left Ireland. He had previously had triple bypass surgery and wasn't allowed to fly. So I booked my flight and told him I was coming to see him.

I left Adam with my mother and took a 12-hour flight to San Francisco. Mam didn't approve of my plan, although part of her was curious to see how my father was. She knew there was no point trying to stop me.

When I arrived in the city, I turned on my phone to find a message from my dad, cancelling our meeting the following day. He wasn't feeling well, he said. I was gutted. But I called him back and told him I was coming anyway. He told me he didn't believe I had come all that way just to see him, and he was sure I was over to visit some man. Hadn't I better things to do? I begged him and finally convinced him to change his mind.

My hotel was in the middle of San Francisco – in a beautiful part of the city. It was one of the nicest places I'd ever stayed in. The next day, after treating myself to a luxurious breakfast, I asked the receptionist to call me a cab to take me to the address my father had given me.

We travelled further and further out of the city centre through areas that were becoming more derelict and run-down with every kilometre. I was nervous and worried and wished the driver was more talkative. I had been hoping he'd ask me where I was going and why, but we drove in silence. As we drove into one particularly dilapidated area, past a homeless shelter, I crossed my fingers that we would be driving on through. Instead, the taxi driver began to slow down. 'Are we far away?' I asked. 'We're here now,' he replied.

I asked him to stop the car immediately. I wanted to get out before we reached the apartment building, so I'd have time to gather myself. As we pulled over, we saw a man on the street, clearly looking for someone.

The moment I saw him, I knew this man would never have been able to be the saviour I had wanted him to be. He was dishevelled and filthy, waxy faced and unkempt. The photographs I had seen were of a skinny, mischievous-looking rocker. This man, lumbering around the road, was much larger and, to be honest, a little scary looking. The taxi driver asked me if I was sure I wanted to get out. I wasn't. Inside, I was saying to myself, 'Please don't let this man be my dad, please …' but I forced myself to open the car door. My dad recognised me immediately and started to cry.

We hugged, kind of awkwardly, and went to a nearby coffee shop. He kept staring at me. I had, as usual, dressed up for what for me was an important moment – my first proper meeting with my own father. I'd taken care over what I wore and how I looked. I was wearing my best clothes; I'd had my hair done. His clothes were ripped, torn and dirty. He turned this against me, using it as a way to criticise me from the start, accusing me of being overly materialistic and focused on my appearance. He kept talking and talking. For the first time in my life, I couldn't get a word in edgeways. He didn't ask me many questions about my life. Instead, he told me about himself and then he told me what he thought about me. Eventually, he asked me to come back to his apartment for a while. Reluctantly, I agreed.

On the short walk to his apartment, he was very emotional and not quite with it. But he was happy too. He knew the women outside the homeless shelter by name and proudly announced to them 'This is my daughter!'

Inside the flat, my eyes were well and truly opened. The space was dark, gloomy and cluttered. There were shelves full of medication, and he told me he was still on methadone. Books and papers were strewn all over the floors. Dishes were piled high in the kitchen sink. There was a musty smell in the air.

In the midst of the clutter and the rubbish, however, were a few reminders of the younger man my mam had fallen for. His electric guitars were on the wall in the sitting room, alongside a Buddhist shrine. On the kitchen table lay scraps of unfinished poems and songs. He gave me some poetry books and some poems he said he had written especially for me. In the spare room, speakers and other recording equipment were stacked from floor to ceiling.

Now, instead of wanting to be saved, I wanted to save him. The moment I met him, I became the parent. I wanted to protect him, to 'fix' him, aesthetically, physically, medically, mentally. I went over there thinking I was going to have a daddy who would protect me. Instead, I found a broken man who needed his own protector. I had a dream that I could get him back to Ireland and my mother could be reunited with her long-lost love. They would be two artistic souls together! Mam would have killed me, of course, even if I could have made this childish fantasy a reality. She had worked long and hard to get her life back on track. My father was still grappling with his addiction.

It was all quite overwhelming, and I headed back to my nice hotel for the night. We arranged to meet again the following day. I wanted to visit Alcatraz, the site of the infamous prison, and my dad said he'd come with me. I booked tickets and made all the arrangements, but at the last minute he cancelled, and I ended up spending the day on my own. He told me he was too sick to come and again suggested that I hadn't made the trip just to see him and said he was sure I'd find other people to hang out with. I was devastated, but in some ways a little relieved. I was finding it hard to accept how he looked and how unwell he clearly was. I had booked an open return ticket, but that evening, sitting on my own in a restaurant near Alcatraz as the sun went down, I booked my ticket home, to leave in less than a week.

I think now that I panicked a little, that I should have given it more time. It had been my dream all my life to meet my daddy and for my daddy to want me. I feel I should have seen more of him. It was only towards the end of my trip that we began to bond a little more. I was watching him – his movements, his features – and seeing myself in him. I was leaving when our relationship had only just started.

On my last morning, he took me for breakfast. I wanted to go shopping with him. I wanted to buy him new clothes and a smartphone so we could stay in touch over FaceTime. He wouldn't let me buy him a phone but he promised he'd get one himself. He had brought one of his guitars with him, which he asked me to take home for Adam, and as I said goodbye, he pushed a wad of notes – around $300 – into my hand. I didn't want to take his money – I knew he didn't have much – but he insisted. My mam later said I shouldn't feel bad about taking it, as it was the only such gift he'd ever given me. That made me feel a bit better. I was also relieved to see that he did have some money and reassured that he would keep his promise to get the phone and keep in contact.

When I got home, my mam listened patiently as I outlined

my plans to have a relationship with my dad and to get the man she'd last seen almost 30 years previously over to Ireland. I knew he couldn't fly, but I was convinced I would find some way to make it happen. I waited for him to call me, but the call never came. I thought I was going to America to find a father who would be with me for the rest of my life, but he disappeared on me again. Eventually I managed to get hold of him, and he sounded annoyed that he hadn't heard from me. He told me it was my fault and that I was supposed to stay in touch with him. I didn't get angry because, of course, I also blamed myself. He was right – it was my fault. I believed I should have made more effort with him. I shouldn't have been embarrassed about the way he looked or acted. I should have contacted him more. Each time we've spoken since, it has been me who has reached out.

It's taken a lot for me not to let the lack of interaction break my heart, but I tell myself these days that I'm over it. Men have caused a lot of hurt in my life. And I blame myself for much of it. I'm still amazed when a man shows compassion for me. I feel I don't deserve it, yet I'm flattered by it. That worries me! I know there are nice men out there. I have watched men I have dated with their kids and seen the beautiful way they interact with them. But I feel I've grown in the years since my trip to the USA and that I am much more independent. I am a mother to a wonderful son, and I think

I'm almost over the hopeless longing for a proper relationship with my own dad.

10

SHAME

When I saw the first campaign poster, it was like getting punched in the face. I took it personally. I shouldn't have been shocked. I knew this referendum was coming. But the poster sent me right back to 2007. I was standing once again outside the High Court, facing protesters who were accusing me of wanting to kill a disabled child.

In April 2018, I was working in a clothes shop in Drogheda. I had a senior position, responsible for rosters and cash lodgements. The posters had gone up that morning all around the town and were lining my route to the bank. This one was almost identical to those carried by the pro-life campaigners outside the High Court. It showed a close-up photograph of a foetus in the womb, with the words 'A licence to kill? Vote No to abortion on demand'. I had to lean against a shopfront to catch my breath. The last time I had seen an image like that, it had been waved in front of my face 11 years previously.

The vote on whether to remove the special protection for the unborn from the constitution had been set for 25 May 2018. The 'No' campaigners, were first to get their posters up as the campaign got underway. Abortion was such a controversial and divisive issue in the country that politicians had been trying their best for years to avoid dealing with it. When my court case ended, I felt the issues it raised had been quickly swept under the carpet as I was whisked off to Liverpool. Even on the day the judge made his decision, politicians were quick to rule out any possibility of bringing in new legislation to deal with the subject.

The Minister for Justice at the time, Michael McDowell, welcomed the ruling in my case, but when he was asked if something should be done to ensure a similar situation would not happen again, he refused to discuss the abortion issue while a general election campaign was under way. Mary Harney, the then Minister for Health, said she did not believe the issue would be revisited by politicians for a long time to come. She said the debate was dominated by extremes and no government wanted to commit to introducing legislation.

I suppose their lack of enthusiasm about tackling such a difficult issue wasn't surprising. But despite their reluctance, the awkward cases kept surfacing over the following years – cases involving women put in impossible situations, where their fates were decided by the eighth amendment to the constitution. The politicians couldn't avoid it any longer, and in 2018, they finally took action. The people were going to be asked if the special protection, guaranteeing unborn children in the womb an equal right to life with their mothers, should be removed.

I had spoken out publicly about some of these other cases. About a month before Christmas 2009, I got a call from the solicitor who had acted for me in the Miss D case. Conor told me an RTÉ reporter called Keelin Shanley wanted to talk to me and asked if I'd be willing to meet her. He said she wanted to interview me on the *Prime Time* current affairs programme about the court cases coming up in Europe.

I pretended to know what he was talking about, and I told him I would think about talking to the reporter. In the meantime, I thought I had better find out more. I couldn't believe what I read. Three women who had travelled to the UK to have abortions were taking Ireland to the European Court of Human Rights for not allowing them to have terminations in their own country. What struck me was that these women were all described as letters of the alphabet, just like me. They were known as A, B and C, and they claimed they had been traumatised and their health put in danger because they hadn't been able to have the abortions in their own country.

One of the women had addiction issues and suffered from depression. She had other children in care and was worried another pregnancy would damage her chances of getting them back. The second woman had become pregnant even though she had taken the morning-after pill. She did not feel she could care for a child and was concerned about the risk of having an ectopic pregnancy. The third woman had a rare form of cancer. She had tests before she found out she was pregnant and could not get reassurance that her unborn child would not be damaged by these tests and that her health would not be put at risk by the pregnancy.

As I read more, I discovered that I was not even the first Miss D. The year before my case had ended up in the High Court, another woman, known as D, had taken Ireland to court in Europe. She had been carrying twins. One died in the womb, and the other had a fatal foetal abnormality, almost as severe as Jasmine's. She, like me, had opted to have a medical induction in a hospital in the UK. She had argued in Europe that she should have been able to have an abortion in Ireland.

D lost her case for reasons that were familiar to me. The state successfully persuaded the European court that she hadn't done everything she could have done to fight her case in Ireland first. Lawyers for the state had argued that if she had gone to the Irish High Court, before going to Europe, the judge might have accepted her child was not 'unborn' under the law and was not protected because it had no chance of survival. They argued she might have been able to have had her termination in Ireland after all. That was the same argument put forward by my lawyers in the High Court a year later, but it made little difference. It was a question the judge felt was not necessary for him to decide in my case.

My heart ached when I read the details of the other women's cases. I was still embarrassed to be Miss D and to be publicly associated with abortion. But this made me think there were many more people in similar situations than I had realised.

I was also angry that our lives as women were subject to such control. Women were expected to just do what we were told, in my view. If we wanted to fight back and challenge the authorities, we had to be willing to get lawyers, go to court and put our lives on public display. Lots of women wouldn't be in a position to do that. I decided I would do the interview with the reporter. What's more, I decided I wouldn't do it anonymously: I would show my face.

I thought long and hard about this. But I knew that when you hear a story without seeing the face of the person telling it, it makes it harder to connect with the situation. I wanted people to connect with me. I thought that showing my face might make it a bit more real for people who were still ignorant about what was going on. I hated people knowing all about my business. But I was also sick of cowering and becoming upset when people pointed and whispered and wondered if I was Miss D. I was going to announce it, in public, and say 'Yes! It is me!' I felt something good would come from it.

Keelin and the team were very kind to me, and the interview went out in December 2009. I was still only a baby, just 19 years old. I was nervous and passionate about my subject, and my strong emotions came across clearly on screen. I was only at the beginning of my battle with my shame and my own feelings about abortion. I told Keelin I did not agree with people who had abortions 'just because' they didn't want a baby. But I said people like me should not be made to feel like murderers. We should get help and support in Ireland, I said, instead of having to travel.

A year later, the European Court of Human Rights gave its ruling and found that Ireland had breached the rights of one of the three women. Keelin rang me again, and I was enthusiastic about going back on television to talk about the issues.

I was petrified each time about the kind of reaction I was going to get. But I needn't have worried. The support I received surprised me. I didn't feel like people were judging me from a 'pro-life' or 'pro-choice' point of view. People seemed to understand the decision I had made. When I came back into class the day after my second interview, I was apprehensive about what the other girls would say. It helped that lots of them were not regular viewers of current affairs programmes and hadn't seen it. That meant the reaction was less overwhelming and I didn't have to talk about it constantly. But the girls who had seen me, or had heard about the interview, were extremely supportive and surprised.

I was seen in my class as loud and sassy. The persona I was used to putting on was of someone who had loads of confidence and attitude, hiding the insecurity I felt inside. I was just starting to get into modelling and promotional work, and I seemed to be someone who hadn't a care in the world. Some of the other girls had probably been wondering who the hell I thought I was. It came as a shock to them to hear about my past and to understand a little about the circumstances that had made me the person I was.

During lunch break, a girl approached me. She was a little younger than me and was one of those who had come straight onto the course after leaving school. We didn't get on particularly well. Like some of the others, she probably thought my ego was a little out of control! That day, however, the girl told me she had actually studied my case during a social studies class in school and she remembered it well. She was surprised to find Miss D had actually been sitting beside her in college, learning how to wax eyebrows and apply shellac nail polish. Her entire attitude towards me changed.

Her name was Sarah, and from that day on, she became one of my closest friends, as well as a very important part of Adam's life. We speak all the time, and I'm grateful to have such a good friend who understands some of what I've experienced.

I was happy for a while in my little bubble in college, but as the months went on, my head went down again in shame. I started to focus on the negative comments I saw more than the positive support I had received. I fixated on the people who were saying I had killed my baby or that I was doing interviews on television for the money. I knew that some people believed I was getting paid every time I spoke publicly. But for me it had nothing to do with money. It was a serious issue that I felt passionately about. Yet I was being made to feel as if I was looking for something in return.

I decided I wasn't going to speak in public any more. I had to get on with my life: I had a son to rear. I didn't want to be known for ever as Miss D or the 'abortion girl'. Try as I might, however, I could not escape my past.

The first time it happened, it confirmed everything for me – all my paranoia, all my anxiety, all my shame. I was sitting on the couch with the guy I was seeing at the time. We were watching a movie when he got a text. He turned to me and showed me the message on his phone. It read: 'Watch yourself, you don't know who you're dating.' 'What's all this about?' he asked. His phone pinged again with a picture of me in an article about the *Prime Time* interview and the court case accompanied by a headline about Miss D.

My past had affected me in all my relationships since I had broken up with Adam's dad. It was always in the back of my mind when I met someone. I felt that I had to make a choice every time – should I back away from the situation before I got too close and ended up getting hurt? Or should I bring up my past and make a joke about it myself before the other person heard about me from someone else?

I was too late to get there first with this guy. And I wasn't sure how to react to the texts he had received. Did he mind? Would he think it was a big deal? Would he think I had done something wrong? I could tell from the tone of his voice, as he asked me questions, that he wasn't impressed and didn't want to deal with the issues raised by my answers. It was just too much baggage to handle, and we broke up shortly afterwards.

I was a young single mother – that alone made it hard to meet people. But in my case, I was also carrying around my grief for my dead child and dragging a big, controversial debate about abortion along for good measure. It was not exactly attractive. What young man would want to deal with that?

I felt I was disgusting to men, and I disgusted myself. It makes me sad even to write those words, to see in black and white how much I hated myself. People would never have guessed this from the way I acted. I was a part-time model; I looked good and took care of myself. The 17-year-old in the grey tracksuit with the scraped-back hair had long been banished. I was super glamorous, always dressed well and was constantly changing my image. I had a comfortable home and a wonderful son. But I didn't like myself. My over-riding emotion was always shame.

I had felt ashamed of myself and my life since the evening we had arrived in Drogheda. I was ashamed we were living in a women's refuge. Later, I became ashamed that my dad wasn't around, that we were renting our home. I was ashamed of Mam's drinking, ashamed of our rows. When the court case happened, I felt my shame was on public display for everyone to see. I was ashamed that the whole country knew I was in care. And I was deeply ashamed that I was being mentioned in the same breath as abortion. Even though I knew I had no choice but to terminate my pregnancy with Jasmine, a part of me still felt guilty about it. I couldn't seem to climb out of this hole of shame and embarrassment, despite the front I put on for the world.

Maybe it was so difficult to move on because abortion was just not something that anyone wanted to talk about.

Certainly, no one I knew talked about it on a personal level. I had never had those conversations. And I didn't personally know anyone else who had gone through anything like my experience.

On the rare occasions that the subject came up in college or in work, I couldn't help but take it all extremely personally. I saw any discussion about abortion as an argument about my life and about the decisions I had made. I would become extremely angry and extremely passionate, trying to make people see my point of view. I stepped in even when the conversation didn't involve me at all. I didn't think anyone else could give a better insight into the issue than me.

When it first became clear that there was going to be another vote on abortion, I wanted to leave the country. The issue was again starting to dominate every radio show, every news programme. I just did not think I could handle being dragged back into my past, into a time when it felt as if the whole country had a view on my pregnancy, my baby and my choice.

At the same time as the referendum campaign was just starting to ramp up, I was still dealing with aftershocks from my 2007 court case. There was still unfinished legal business.

In 2010, I had begun a legal action against the HSE for the

pain and distress their actions had caused me. I didn't really have a strong desire to go after anyone in the courts, but my mam recommended a new solicitor to me, and he told me I had to act quickly. If I didn't lodge a case within two years of my 18th birthday, I wouldn't be able to do it at all.

I gave him the go-ahead to initiate the case. My claim alleged that the HSE had been responsible for my welfare but that they had failed to look after me physically and psychologically, that they'd caused me distress and anxiety and had destroyed my trust in them. The court documents outlined that I had been experiencing extreme symptoms of stress and anxiety since 2007 and that I frequently had panic attacks as well as symptoms of depression.

Nothing much happened for several years. The case bubbled along without appearing to get very far. Every so often, I would get a phone call from the solicitor asking me to authorise certain actions; I had to be assessed again by psychiatrists; and then it would all go quiet for another period of time.

In late 2017, however, the case sprang back to life. There was talk of a trial date, where we would argue the issues, in full, before a High Court judge. Then, at the beginning of March 2018, I got a call telling me to come to court a few days later, when there would be discussions between both sides to try to reach a settlement.

As my mother and I made our way back through the gates of the Four Courts for the first time in 11 years, there were no camera crews, angry protesters or distressing placards waiting for us. I hadn't forgotten those days, though, and when I met my solicitor beside the barristers' library in the heart of the old building, I was angry, and I wanted to fight. I was told, however, that a settlement would be in my best interests. We were there to negotiate and to avoid a court case. Mam and I were brought to a consultation room to wait.

Throughout the morning, my lawyers shuttled back and forth between our room and that of the HSE's legal team.

The talks started off with the possibility of a reasonably large settlement. In my head I thought I would get as much as €100,000. But as the negotiations continued, the figure kept decreasing. I was insulted and distraught. Was this all I was worth? Even worse, was this all Jasmine was worth?

At some point, it became clear to me that if we didn't reach an agreement, and the matter went to court, I would be all over the newspapers and television news bulletins once again. I can't remember if that suggestion came from my solicitor, whether it was a point made to him by the HSE's lawyers, or whether I had just managed to work it out on my own. It scared me but, of course, it was the truth. There was bound to be publicity if there was another court battle between Miss D and the HSE all these years later.

I was terrified that any publicity would mean that my relationship with my mother would be dragged through the news again. Just when it seemed we had reached a good point in our lives, we could be destroyed. I believed I would be publicly embarrassed and shamed just as I had been in 2007.

What I didn't realise at the time is how much public opinion would have been on my side. I didn't take into account that the HSE would not have welcomed the publicity either. The judgment in 2007 very clearly identified what the HSE had done wrong and was very critical about certain actions that had been taken. Furthermore, they would not have been enthusiastic about fighting me in court in a year where the position of women who had to travel for abortions was coming under such a bright spotlight. But, of course, at that stage I hadn't yet read the judgment. I didn't realise the bargaining power I had on my side, and I was losing my stomach for a court battle.

The negotiations didn't last as long as I thought they should have. In the end, we settled for about half of what was originally discussed, and my legal costs were also paid. The lawyers went into the High Court, the judge was told a settlement had been reached and the case was struck out, for ever.

I had grand dreams that I would use some of my settlement money to fund medical research into anencephaly. Instead, I had just enough to sort out my life and pay off some loans. It wasn't that I wanted lots of money from the HSE, although in the High Court that is really the only way to make your point. What I wanted was for the extent of the wrong that had been done to me to be recognised. More importantly than anything else, I wanted someone to say, 'Amy, we're sorry things happened the way they did.'

I didn't think the money I received came anywhere close to acknowledging how deeply I had been affected by the court battle, and I never got an apology. Less than a month later, the date for the repeal referendum was set. If I had been able to wait until the votes were counted, I think the HSE would have been negotiating with a much stronger woman, and the outcome might have been different.

It was only around a month after the settlement when I spotted that first poster on the lamppost in Drogheda. The events of 2007 were, therefore, very much on my mind. I already had one foot in the past, in the most traumatic period of my life.

As the weeks went on, the posters became more numerous, and their message became more oppressive to me. It got to the stage that I would have an emotional crisis every time I went out for a coffee. There seemed to be many more posters supporting the pro-life campaign than the pro-choice side, and all of them seemed to be passing judgement directly on me. 'Babies will die, vote pro-life, vote no,' one proclaimed. Another said, 'In England 1 in 5 babies are aborted. Don't bring this to Ireland. Vote No.' There were photographs of foetuses. And there was a photograph of a baby in the womb with the message 'I am nine weeks old. I can yell and kick. Don't Repeal Me.' I immediately thought of Jasmine's perfectly formed hands and feet. I walked past dozens of these posters every day. There were ads on the radio and television, discussions on every programme. I felt like I was being swallowed up by the debate – I couldn't escape it.

Adam was ten years old at the time, curious and interested in everything that was going on. He was seeing the posters too, and he started to ask me all kinds of questions. He didn't know at the time what the word 'abortion' really meant, but he knew there was some kind of connection with me. I had previously told him about Jasmine, his older sister who had died.

One afternoon, on the way home from school, he told me that abortion was 'sick'. I felt like bursting into tears, but I had to try to explain the posters, the referendum and my own past in a way that a young child could understand. We sat in traffic as I tried to explain that Jasmine had not been 'murdered'. I told him that she had been very ill and that having her inside my body had started to make me ill too, and that was the reason she had needed to come out. He understood it was something I had to do. At some level, I think he understood that he probably wouldn't even exist if I hadn't been able to do what I did. I told him I had to go to England, which made me very upset, and the vote was to decide if things like that could happen in Ireland.

It wasn't a conversation I wanted to have with him at all at that age. When I was ten, I knew absolutely nothing about abortion. But the topic had become impossible to avoid. I also thought I needed to explain to him why I was becoming sadder and more upset as the campaign went on. He needed to know it had nothing to do with him.

As we got closer to 25 May, conversations about the referendum, abortion and women's bodies were becoming more common. It was now almost part of our daily chit-chat at work. From an issue that had rarely been discussed when I was growing up, and even in the years since my court case, it was now something we were all talking about, almost as easily as we discussed the weather or whether we liked the fit of the new black jackets we had in stock.

I worked with a small bunch of women in the shop. We all came from diverse backgrounds and had been brought up with different beliefs, yet every day we were learning from each other and changing our opinions as we heard other people's stories.

One of the girls had only recently joined the team. Leanne

and I got on very well, and one evening as we tidied up the rails of clothes, we got talking. I had noticed she was wearing a small badge with the word 'repeal' on her top, and she had never made any secret of the fact that she was campaigning for a Yes vote. I had been dying to get a chance to talk to her in detail, as I thought she would understand what I had been through. I asked her about her badge and mentioned to her that I had lost a child. The details came flooding out after that – Jasmine, the court case, Liverpool. She stared at me open-mouthed, and when I'd finished talking she didn't say anything, she just hugged me.

Leanne was very involved in the campaign in Drogheda to repeal the eighth amendment. She went to every march and fundraiser, and she made it her mission to get me involved too. We used to go to the bingo nights together. I've no idea why a campaign to change the constitution featured so many bingo nights, but they were really fun and enjoyable events. Lots of young people always went and, surprisingly to me, plenty of men too. Sometimes the men outnumbered the women! I was starting see exactly how much support was out there.

She tried to get me to come with her to the big rallies in Dublin. I wanted to. I would tell her that I would go, but I would always back out at the last minute. I was genuinely frustrated, and sometimes I would be convinced that I could manage it. I'd be excited in the days leading up to the rally.

But that excitement was always tinged with dread. I felt marches and rallies with big crowds were something I would just not be able to handle. I was afraid of the atmosphere, of being overwhelmed. My shame and my anger were just too strong. When I passed groups of campaigners in my own town, standing near the church with pro-life leaflets laid out in front of them on tables, I had to fight the urge to kick over the tables and scatter the leaflets. I didn't feel I could trust my emotions at a rally with thousands of people. Even today, I'm not sure I would be able to handle such an event.

I was contacted by pro-choice campaigners and encouraged to share my experience publicly. I didn't feel I could. I was willing to wear badges and jumpers and play bingo. But I didn't want to get up in front of a roomful of people, or even a microphone, as Miss D. Eventually, I agreed to give an interview to a journalist from the BBC who was putting together a piece for their website. It consumed a lot of my time, as she came back to me on several occasions over the weeks leading up to the vote to get my views. I felt that by doing the interview I was playing my part, even if I wasn't out waving banners. It was all I could do.

I was taking this campaign more personally than ever. I knew it wasn't all about me. I knew it was about every woman in the country. I was annoyed at myself for feeling the way I did. I thought I was being selfish and self-centred, and I kept telling myself to pull myself together. But inside my head, I felt it was a referendum about Miss D. Every day I was reminded of what had happened to me. I was reminded of Jasmine and the circumstances of her birth. I was constantly reliving the trauma.

I was also feeling rage – not just at what I had been through, but that so many women had also had to go through the same in the years since my case. They may not have had the added stress of a court case, but they understood what it was like to carry a baby who wouldn't live, to leave that child in another country, and to wait sadly at home for their child's body or even their ashes to be sent back to them. I felt my case in 2007 should have been a turning point, a chance for the state to do something for all these women. Yet 11 years later nothing had changed. The fact that I was a young girl who was in care at the time overshadowed all the other issues. The devastation of what happened after I went to Liverpool was overlooked.

I was crying a lot, at home and at work. I became addicted to reading the stories of women who had travelled for abortions, outlined on a Facebook page called 'In Her Shoes'. I spent my lunchbreaks in tears, scrolling through the stories.

It was through reading these accounts that my own viewpoint started to change. I began to understand that I was not alone, that I had never been alone. Other women had been in situations like mine, or in positions I considered to be far worse. I know it seems hard to believe, but I just did not comprehend how many others were affected. There were women who had been abused, women who had been raped, women who couldn't afford to have a child, women who had cancer and had to choose between carrying a child or trying to stay alive. Suddenly, they were all telling their stories. To me, they were all Miss Ds. They were all women in difficult and sometimes desperate circumstances, and there were so many of us. There weren't just two or three exceptional cases: there were thousands.

The story that stayed with me longest was that of a woman who already had one child and was being treated for cancer when she found out she was pregnant. Her doctors had advised her to have a termination. But the hospital she was attending refused to carry out the termination in Ireland, under the existing law, because there was 'no immediate risk' to her life. She ended up having to put in place arrangements to travel to the UK for an abortion. She couldn't have treatment until she had had the abortion, and she later died from her cancer. I felt her case was much more important than mine had ever been. She had a husband and a child who needed her.

The day of the result is a blur. I remember being anxious. I was vaguely aware there had been an exit poll the night before predicting that the Yes side had won, decisively. But I wasn't willing to believe it until there was an official announcement.

I asked my mam to come around to watch the result with me on the news. She was almost as nervous as I was. But she told me she had never felt shame about my decision and had always supported me and my right to choose. There was never anything to be ashamed of, she told me. She too had found the campaign difficult and had been reliving the court case every time she saw the graphic posters.

As the six o'clock news got closer, I felt as if I was back in the B&B, waiting on a phone call from my solicitor. It was as if I was going to get my answer from the judge all over again. If the change to the constitution was rejected, it would mean that my choices had also been rejected. It would be a signal that the majority of people believed what I had done was wrong. It was a verdict on what I had chosen to do.

The announcement came just after 6.15 p.m. on 25 May: 66.4 per cent of people had voted Yes; 33.6 per cent had voted no. The eighth amendment to the constitution, protecting the equal right to life of the 'unborn', was gone. I was stunned. It wasn't even close! Mam and I hugged each other, ecstatic and utterly relieved. Our smiles of joy quickly turned into relieved sobs as we took in the enormity of what had happened. I hadn't been aware so much of the country was on my side.

For 11 years, I had felt like a murderer, like a bad person who had to be made an example of. I had worried that every time I shared a piece of my story I was encouraging people to have abortions, and that this was wrong in almost every situation. I was sad that I had lost so many years to useless guilt and embarrassment. My mental health had suffered so much from years of feeling depressed and repressed. And there was no need for any of it. The dark cloud of shame was beginning to lift, and I could see myself as I really was.

The result changed my life. It was the beginning of a huge change in my attitude. I just wished it had happened much, much earlier. At the same time, both my mam and myself were also wary. We wondered how the result of the referendum would actually be put into effect.

That night, I thought about how my life had turned out. If things had gone differently, if I hadn't been in care, or maybe even if I'd spoken to a different social worker or hadn't told the HSE at all, there might never have been a court case or a public controversy. I could have gone to England as soon as I found out about Jasmine's condition. I could have had the procedure I needed to have and got on with the rest of my life. I'm sure I would have thought about the abortion from time to time, and I would still have had to deal with the grief, but I don't think it would have had such a defining effect on me. Most importantly, my private tragedy could have stayed private.

If I'd been allowed to have the termination in Ireland, I would have been looked after in my own community. The only people who would have known about my circumstances would have been my close friends and family. I wouldn't have spent weeks on end researching abortions and agonising about travelling. I wouldn't have been in court or all over the media.

But the path I was forced to take meant I had to make a connection with Jasmine. Her flutters in my stomach made her a real baby to me. I had to have regular scans and hear her heart beating. I didn't just have a 'procedure': I gave birth to a child and then had to abandon her in another country. I had to pick a coffin and plan a funeral. I have a grave to visit, a box of memories, a scrapbook full of newspaper cuttings, a Wikipedia entry. My son has a sister.

There's a part of me that wishes I had been allowed to take that first path, a part that wishes I had never made that connection with Jasmine. And yet, in other ways, I'm grateful for it. I have a guardian angel and I found resilience and strength in myself that I would never have known otherwise. I just wish it could have been my own choice.

My birthday will always remind me of the worst day of my life: the day I found out my daughter had anencephaly. I have other dates scarred onto my heart now as well: the day I gave birth to Jasmine, the day we buried her, the day she was due to be born.

I'm proud of myself and how I dealt with it all. But it's

interesting to wonder what my life would be like now, if Miss D had never existed. Everything might be completely different.

11

I AM AMY DUNNE

The studio lights were hot on my face. The audience members were looking at me expectantly as the host, Claire Byrne, asked me a question. It was November 2019, more than a year since the referendum.

Claire was asking me if I was defined by what had happened to me. 'I am not Miss D, the victim,' I said. 'I am Miss D, a strong and powerful woman!'

Claire interrupted me immediately. 'Well,' she said, 'you're Amy Dunne.' What followed was the corniest moment of my life and, unfortunately for me, it was live on national television. 'Yes!' I said, or rather, I shouted. 'I'm AMY DUNNE! I'm AMY DUNNE! And I've a lot going on in my life, and I've a lot going for me!'

The audience applauded, and afterwards in the green room for guests on the show, my little sister Claire, who had come with me to the studio, gave me a big hug. When I watched it back myself the next day, I couldn't stop cringing, but what I had said was true. I hadn't planned it, and for one moment I had forgotten about the television cameras. Sitting in the courtroom in 2007, I felt powerless and voiceless. I never got a chance to speak or to give evidence. Now, I wanted to use my voice as much as possible, loudly and publicly.

At the end of 2018, I was contacted by a team who were making a documentary series for the Irish language channel TG4. The series, called *Finné,* or 'witness', was about people who had gone through traumatic, newsworthy or historic events telling their stories directly to camera, from their own perspective. I agreed to take part, and making it was like getting rid of a huge, heavy burden of rubbish that had been sitting in my brain. I felt I was regaining my voice and my story.

We did hours of interviews. I brought the team all around Drogheda and showed them where I spent my teenage years. We went to the hill above the town and to my old school, as well as to the dark house in the factory grounds. The windows of the house were bricked up, and the garden was a tangled mess of grass and weeds. Amazingly, over in a corner, in among the nettles, I saw a flash of pink and spotted the Barbie jeep I had loved to play with as a young girl. It had been abandoned there when we left that place, along with the rest of my childhood innocence. I took it home and cleaned it up, delighted to have a memory of the child I had once been.

Of course, the programme couldn't broadcast every single word of what I said to the team, but my words weren't edited as much as they had been in other interviews I had given. It was the truest representation of my life I had ever put out publicly, until now.

The reaction to the documentary stunned me. It was nice to be myself and to be liked for who I was. As well as Claire Byrne's television show, I was also asked onto a major morning show on RTÉ Radio One. The interview pushed me way outside my comfort zone. The presenter, Sean O'Rourke, asked me my views on the result of the referendum and what I thought about pro-life protesters gathering outside hospitals where abortions were being carried out. It was a strange feeling for me to be discussing these kinds of issues with one of the top current affairs presenters in the country, but I wasn't afraid and I spoke from my heart. No one should be allowed to protest outside a hospital, I told him, and they should not be allowed to gather outside hospitals to pray either. No one knows why a woman has made the decision to end a pregnancy, and it is not something anyone takes lightly, I said. I had changed my views totally since I was a 17-year-old girl. I no longer felt that ending a pregnancy was something to feel shame about.

During that interview, Sean asked me if I had received support or counselling during the years since the court case. He could see me becoming emotional as I spoke to him, and I could hear real concern in his voice. I had been promised counselling, and even the obstetrician who had provided a report for the court had said I would need the best of medical and psychological care. In the years that followed, however, that hadn't really happened.

Since I was around 12 years old, I've tried to counsel myself. When I had no reliable adult around, I acted as my own parent and tried to guide myself through difficult situations. I've had so many different adult figures in my life. There have been social workers, teachers, foster parents. I tried to learn a little from everyone I came across. I adopted their good qualities, as much as I could, and I tried not to develop characteristics that I didn't like.

That approach worked well enough for me for a long time. But the process of writing this book reopened lots of old wounds, some that I thought were completely healed.

Speaking on television and radio about Miss D was easier than analysing my entire life. In interviews I was asked a lot about the court case and about the facts of what happened to me during that short space of time in 2007. I became so used to it that, most of the time, I didn't really feel the grief as I spoke. It was like a story I was telling about someone else.

In contrast, every single bit of reliving my story and pinning down the details for posterity has been difficult. Even thinking about my happy childhood and the good times I had with my mother hurts me. It all ended so abruptly, and it was such a loss to me when it was gone that I feel grief when I think about those times, not joy. Writing about the court case was almost the easy part. Recognising everything else that I have been through and doing my best to face it head on has been intense and exhausting.

I feel like I've been broken down and am in the process of building myself back up, brick by brick. I've come to terms with heartache I had never really dealt with and faced traumas I had tried to store in a compartment in my brain. It's true that I should probably have done this years ago, with a psychiatrist, but I've never found someone I felt comfortable with. Some of those I went to over the years had no idea how to deal with my specific situation. In some counselling sessions that I attended early on, I had to explain my story right from the beginning. I'd even have to explain to the counsellor exactly what anencephaly was. By the time I had finished that, I would be so drained I wouldn't see the point of continuing or feel like saying any more.

At times, during this process, I've felt like crumbling. I haven't been able to sleep, and I've been very depressed. I know I've taken my emotions out on the people around me, on those I am closest to. It's hard for people to understand why I'm so upset about 'my book' without explaining to them how I feel about all the situations I've been making myself face up to. And that's a lot for anyone to have to listen to! Where would I start?

What I have noticed is that no matter how many times I relive my experience, no matter how many times I tell my story or how detached I become from certain parts of it, there is one point that always catches me. Whenever I talk about leaving Jasmine behind in Liverpool, about the fact that I didn't get a chance to hold her or see her properly, I still fall apart. That scar is always there, never fully healed, just waiting for me to scratch at it. I close my eyes and I can still smell the hospital. I can still remember my devastation and my grief.

It shocked me recently to find out that, despite the vote for change in 2018, there are still women in Ireland who are not allowed to take the decision they feel is best for them, and who still have to travel to the UK. Those who don't fit the criteria in the new legislation brought in after the referendum may not be able to have a termination in Ireland. Some women end up travelling because the prognosis for their child is not fully clear. A mother carrying a baby with anencephaly, like Jasmine, is now allowed to have the procedure in Ireland. But there are other conditions where doctors are not able to say with certainty whether or not the baby will survive outside the womb for more than 28 days. Those women often have to travel to the UK and travel home without their babies, just like I did.

The publicity around the referendum and the documentary led to me having to counsel others. People who had been through similar situations frequently messaged me on social media. When I was working in the bar of a hotel in Drogheda, couples would approach me – men and women – and tell me their own stories of having to go to England to end pregnancies in tragic circumstances. I was taking on these stories as if I was actually a qualified counsellor, and I found it quite overwhelming. From hearing their experiences, it's clear that not all those who had to travel to the UK in such circumstances received proper support or counselling when they returned. It wasn't just me. We were expected to put our grief aside and get on with our lives when we got back to Ireland. But no mother easily gets over leaving her baby in another country, or receiving a Jiffy bag full of ashes from a courier or having a body sent home as cargo on an aeroplane.

I have discovered that the trauma doesn't disappear with time. It's true that I'm no longer embarrassed about who I am. But as I get older and have an adult's understanding of the world, I'm more aware than ever that what happened to me was wrong. I may not be as ashamed any more, but I'm still angry.

The anger can appear out of nowhere. One day, while out for a walk, I saw a pro-life sticker on a car parked along the road. I had to be restrained by my friend from ripping it off. When I read Mr Justice McKechnie's judgment for the first time, in the process of writing this book, it also made me furious. It boggled my brain.

The judgment confirmed everything I had said about the case over the years, which was a relief to me. I often second-guess myself, and I wondered sometimes if I had made too big a deal of the things that had happened. Was I being, as usual, overdramatic? I know now that I had actually underestimated what I had gone through. The judgment also confirmed to me that I had ended up in the middle of a circus that should never have been allowed to happen.

I was angered further by what I read at the end of the court's judgment, on the pages at the back of the copy I received. After the judge had made his decision, the stenographer who was taking down his words had to keep going until the court proceedings were finished. She recorded the final exchanges between the lawyers and the judge.

To any objective person reading these conversations, there was nothing wrong with what was said. They spoke about the issue of costs, with the HSE saying its position was that neither my mother nor myself should be expected to pay costs of any kind. Finally, there was some polite discussion between my lawyers and the judge. They thanked him for hearing the case 'with such efficiency'. The judge thanked all the legal teams involved.

This conversation made me irrationally annoyed. While they had been exchanging these pleasantries, I had been sobbing my heart out in the bedroom of a B&B in Slane. It was just another day at the office for them. I was just another case. I know this fury wasn't fair – they were all just being polite. But my life had been affected by every word uttered in that courtroom. How could they just go on with normal everyday life after what had just happened?

It seemed to me that everyone had forgotten the person at the centre of the case. To those in court it was about an awkward constitutional issue that needed to be sorted out quickly, and they were delighted that it was finally, as they saw it, resolved. It seemed to me that only the judge himself was still thinking about me. He realised I still had a hard road to travel. He saw me as the vulnerable 17-year-old girl I was, and for that I am so grateful to him.

His faith in my mother, which she greatly appreciated, paid off. Our relationship wasn't rebuilt overnight. But little by little we started to trust each other again. After I had Adam, Mam reclaimed her mothering role, and she has barely left my side since he turned one. As a young child, I remember a beautiful, caring woman, always affectionate and hands-on emotionally. Adam gave her a sense that she could make up for the lost years with me and be that person again. I lost my daughter but I gained a son and, finally, I got my mammy back.

Our relationship now has never been closer. She feels needed, and there is always something dramatic happening in my life to give her a reason to feel that way! A couple of years ago, I went up to the attic in my house to root out the Christmas decorations, using an ancient ladder that had been in the family for years. As I stepped out of the attic, the ladder collapsed, taking me with it. I fell to the ground and broke my back. I managed to alert my friend Danielle, who rang the guards. In typically dramatic fashion, I was rescued by gardaí, who broke down the door of my house, and I was rushed to hospital by ambulance. My mam was at the hospital within minutes. She stayed with me there and then moved into my house as I recovered. I don't know what I would have done without her, and I was so happy to know I could rely on her. We've travelled on holidays together and we go for dinner regularly. Her support for me and for Adam is the reason I was able to go back to education and why I was able to work. Over the years, she has also managed to rediscover her own creativity. She has taken up painting again, she works with local community groups in Drogheda, and she also makes beautiful herbal soaps.

My mother has told me how proud she is of me for writing this book, and I hope she knows how proud I am of her. I know this process has been almost as difficult for her as it has been for me. Yes, we have laughed a lot, remembering the good times of my childhood – art, performance and dressing up. But I've also had to revisit some of the worst times of our lives and some of the lowest points of our relationship. They are part of my story too. This meant Mam had to be reminded about the most challenging moments of her own life, while she is working hard on continuing to be the loving mother and grandmother she has become in the years since.

My mam and I have had some serious arguments about our memories and about our interpretations of events. She believes my recollections of certain incidents are harder on her than she deserves. She has always said that, even in the darkest days, she idolised me and I was always her little girl.

Being the mother of a teenager myself has given me a new insight into my own teen years. I know a child isn't to blame for what happens to them. But I can see how hard it must have been for my mam to deal with my constant wild, break-free ways, all while she was living in a town where she knew no one and was struggling with her own problems. Those events, which she has been making up for ever since, are difficult for her to see written down in black and white. I know it would hurt me as a mother to read my own child's memories of such a difficult time. I know she still holds a lot of guilt and a lot of anger. And I wish a lot of the craziness hadn't happened. But I hope she knows I don't blame her. And I really hope she can appreciate how far we have come since then.

If I hadn't had Adam, I think everything would have been different for my mother and for me. After having Jasmine, I felt I had very little left to live for. I might have turned to drugs; I might have given up on getting an education. Being gifted a healthy pregnancy so soon after losing Jasmine was a blessing that changed my life.

These days, I'm a little afraid of drink and of drugs. I'll go out and have a drink on a night out. But I rarely drink at home. I'm afraid of the comfort it might bring me. I'm worried that if I drank one night I'd want to drink the next night and the one after that. I saw it happen so slowly and gradually to my mother, in such a completely unintentional, unplanned way. I would be afraid no one would notice I had lost myself until it was too late. So I babysit myself and make sure I don't fall into that hole. I know I have an addictive personality, inherited from both my parents, and I have to be careful.

I've tried to give Adam the most comfortable life I can, while still wanting him to have the same strength and resilience I now have. I would never wish him to experience the chaos and dysfunction of my teenage years, but I want him to have empathy and to know how lucky he is. He has always been very emotionally mature. He has grown up with my loud, straight-talking ways, with my mother alongside him, encouraging him to take an interest in art and nature. He's close to his auntie Claire as well.

Adam has a good attitude to women and to life in general. I've tried to teach him to be polite, gentle and kind and not to look down on others. I've always encouraged him to speak out if he sees injustice happening. And I make sure he stays on the right path.

I'm now dealing with a teenager growing up in the same area where I spent my own difficult teenage years. The difference, I hope, is that I'm able to give him the support and guidance that my mother wasn't always able to give me back then. I know the area and the community well, and I've been through worse teenage traumas than I pray he'll ever experience. He hasn't a hope of pulling the wool over my eyes, as I know every teenage trick in the book. But whether he listens to my guidance or not, I'll support him when he makes mistakes. I'll tell him to enjoy the journey and try not to tell him 'I told you so' during the more difficult times!

I sometimes take him with me to visit his sister's grave. I've visited more than ever before in the past year. I think we're the only people who go there. I sometimes feel I'm the only one who still mourns Jasmine in this way. I feel that people who followed the case didn't fully understand that there was a baby at the end of it. I try to make sure there are fresh plants and flowers on her grave, to make it as pretty as possible. I buy wreaths and spray paint them in different colours to make them more colourful and more glamorous. I would still like to get a bigger, better headstone for her – the one I had wanted with the angel and the heart. But I can't yet face talking to someone about a headstone for my daughter's grave, even after all these years.

There are times when I don't go regularly though, when the flowers wilt and the wreaths fade. I used to feel so guilty about not visiting. I felt as if I was neglecting my daughter. If I walked past the flower aisle while doing the weekly shop and didn't buy a bouquet for Jasmine, or if I bought Adam an expensive present instead of buying something for the grave, I would berate myself. The guilt is gone now, most of the time. I adore and love her, and I feel much more comfortable going up there. If a few weeds are growing on the grave, I try not to punish myself: I dig them up and fix it up again and get on with it.

I don't take out my box of memories as much any more. When I started the process of writing this book, I moved it from over my bed into a cupboard in the spare room. It's not so easily accessible, which means I have to think twice before I open it.

The box used to come down every time I felt low or lost. I used to wallow in my grief. Any time I was upset about anything at all, I would get it down and I would let all the hurt and pain I felt about Jasmine wash over me, even if the reason I was upset to begin with had nothing to do with her. I held her little hospital band; I breathed in the smell of her clothes. It got harder and harder to climb out of that place of sadness once I allowed myself to go into it.

Now, I only open the box when I want to focus on Jasmine, when I really want to remember her and be thankful for what I have now. I am kinder to myself, and I realise I don't have to keep reopening the wound. Just because I don't go to the graveside every day, just because I don't take out her hospital band every night, that doesn't mean I don't love and respect her. I no longer have an urge to dig up her grave. I know she is not up there in that cemetery – she is in my heart.

My emotions can still ambush me out of the blue, however. I was sitting in my car the other day, waiting to pick up Adam when an image of Jasmine in her cot at the hospital popped up on my phone as a memory. I sat there bawling my eyes out, staring at her little fingers and toes.

I have asked myself many times over the years if I should have tried to carry her to full term as some pro-life campaigners had suggested I should. Despite the shame I bore for so long, I never actually regretted what I did. I know it gives comfort to some women in a similar situation to carry on with such pregnancies. I have read about women who found out their babies had anencephaly or other serious conditions and desperately wanted to continue their pregnancies. I've read interviews with women who felt doing so brought them peace and who used the time to make memories and to make plans for the moments after their baby's birth. I respect the decisions those women made. But at my age and in my situation, I am certain that continuing the pregnancy would have brought me nothing but heartache. I had some regrets, and lots of doubts and worries, but I always knew that carrying Jasmine to term, if that had even been possible, would not have been the right thing for me to do. Reading the court's judgment helped me come to terms with that decision. The judge clarified how serious Jasmine's condition was and what the risks to my own health were in a way I hadn't understood before.

I can't imagine having continued with the pregnancy and having people who didn't know me congratulate me and ask when I was due. I can't imagine how it would have affected us and our families to have gone to full term and dealt with the trauma of giving birth to a fully formed child in that condition. I think I would have had nightmares for the rest of my life. I believe I did the right thing for me and for Jasmine.

I honoured her and treated her with as much respect and dignity as I could. More importantly, if I hadn't done what I did, I wouldn't have Adam, and I can't imagine life without him. I have to believe that everything happens for a reason.

I would like to think that after my case hit the headlines no other child in care was treated the way I was treated. At the very least, I don't think any social worker would have wanted the kind of publicity my case attracted. I don't think I would have ended up in court at all if the people who were supposed to be looking after me, and whom I trusted to have my best interests at heart, had treated me more kindly. A hug and a promise that everything would be OK is what I needed, instead of a phone call to the Gardaí to try to stop me leaving the country.

The specific protection in the constitution for the unborn meant that everything was a battle from the beginning. It meant that the law was on the social worker's mind from the moment I told him what had happened and what I planned to do. Even bringing me for a psychiatric assessment was done, I believe, in the hope of guiding me into a situation where I would say I was suicidal. They could have taken more time to work out what to do and how best I could be helped instead of immediately rushing to tell me what I was not allowed to do and trying to make sure the authorities did not allow me to do it.

I wish so much that I'd had more of a voice back then. And I wish my mother and those around me had been able to use their voices too. But it's easy to say that now that I have more confidence and a platform from which to speak. Back then, none of us had that power. We were in desperate circumstances, and we were dependent on the social workers for help. We had no money. I had no proper home. My mam was struggling with alcohol addiction; my boyfriend's mam was raising her kids on her own. We didn't think we could take on the state. We were beaten down by the system that had control of our lives. And we believed, until we were able to consult a solicitor, that we had to do what we were told. No child, no family should have been put in that position. My mother's views should have been taken on board. My best interests should have been the HSE's main consideration.

After my case, the HSE said they had acted on legal advice. They said they had no alternative but to take the actions they took because they believed I needed an order from the district court to be allowed to travel. It was suggested that the ruling in my case would have implications for hundreds of other children in care – that if I was allowed to travel without consent from a court, those children would be able to leave the country whenever they felt like it. That fear seemed to be behind a lot of what the HSE said and did in my case, but it was not borne out. I'm sure other children in care have had to travel to the UK for terminations since 2007, and I hope they were treated with more kindness than I was and received more support than I got.

Writing this book has also made me reflect on my own personality and how I've dealt with the painful episodes in my life. Being a very open, honest person who wears her heart on her sleeve has led to some difficult moments. It's caused me, at times, to trust the wrong people or place too much faith in others, believing that I needed someone to swoop in and save me. I learned the hard way that the father figure I searched for is not going to appear at my door. I learned that my mother's quiet, persistent strength was of more use than my fantasy of a superhero dad. Even still, there are times when I can be overly dazzled by men who show me the slightest hint of compassion or kindness. But as I've written my story, I've realised how strong I have always been and how through the years I have managed to save myself. It was my open, trusting nature that made me tell the HSE that I wanted to go to the UK, hoping they would help me. But it was also my own strength and honesty that got me through the ordeal that followed. I refused to say I was suicidal, and I fought for what I felt was the right thing to do. I came out of a difficult situation, raised my beautiful son and made a life for us

Despite how tough the past few years have been, I know that I am healing and I will be OK. Putting my story together in this book has been part of that process, as traumatic as it may have been. I try now to appreciate the good things that happen in my life. When there is a good moment, I tell myself that it is not immediately going to be followed by something bad. I feel I'm finally putting my past to rest and making space for new growth in my life, even though it's not easy to do. I'm determined not to be defined for ever by what happened in 2007.

I don't hate myself any more or think that I am disgusting. I don't think that I am a burden on those who care about me. I know my survival is a good thing. I'm also pretty sure that anyone I meet should be glad to have someone as strong and resilient as me in their life. I'm thankful for the teachers I met in the Youthreach and Building Your Future programmes, and in college, as well as the individual social workers who supported me and encouraged me to strive to make a better life for myself and my baby.

Adam and I are very close and we talk about everything. I've tried not to burden him with too much information about what happened to me, and why I occasionally appear in the newspapers and on radio and television. When he turned 12 years old, I allowed him to watch the documentary made by the *Finné* team with me. I figured that he was old enough to understand at least some of the issues involved. He didn't say much during the programme. After it was over, he hugged me and told me how brave I was. His beautiful reaction made me cry my eyes out.

There are times when I look at my son and try to visualise what Jasmine might have looked like and what she would be like now. Would she have had the same dark eyes, the same sallow skin, the same thick black hair, the same freckles? Would she have looked as much like me as he does? What kind of daughter would she have been? Would she be into clothes and make-up by now? Would we be going shopping together? Or would she be totally different to me? Would I be standing on the sidelines of a pitch watching her play football or camogie?

I force myself to snap out of it, to stop imagining what might have been. I stood strong and did what I had to do and what was right for me at the time. I've lived through so much, but I am still young and I still have a good life to live.

I don't think I will ever be fully free of my anger about what happened to me as a 17-year-old girl. But these days, I'm looking forward to what the years to come will bring. I want to be able to leave Miss D behind, once and for all, here, on these pages.

ACKNOWLEDGEMENTS

Amy

I'd like to thank everyone who supported and helped me through this whole process:

I would like to thank Orla O'Donnell not only for helping me to write my book but for spending countless hours consoling me through the process as we discussed quite difficult subjects. She always reassured me, and I don't think she will ever know the true comfort I got from her company. It has been tough for both of us – emotionally, mentally and physically – and I truly am ever so grateful.

I'd like to thank Paddy Hayes and Aisling Ní Fhlaithearta, the director and producer of the TG4 series, *Finné*. The programme we made, as well as the reaction to it, completely changed my perception of my situation and set me on the road to accepting who I was.

I want to thank the people behind the 'In My Shoes' Facebook page. I got so much comfort from the stories told on that page. It was the first time it really registered with me that I wasn't alone and that there were so many other women out there with so many similar experiences.

I'd like to thank everyone at Gill Books, especially Sarah Liddy and Aoibheann Molumby, for recognising that my story was an important one to tell while also being so supportive and sensitive with me during the process.

I'm very grateful to the team at work who were so kind and flexible with me.

My best friend Sarah has shared the ups and downs of the last few years of my life with me, and I'm grateful she has put up with me for so long!

The process of writing the book was more emotional than I ever could have imagined, especially with so few other distractions in the last couple of years. I really want to thank the small number of people I've been close to and who have been by my side in that time:

It has been comforting being able to talk about the past with my sisters, Claire and Sharon. Although it was challenging sometimes, it also made us smile as we looked back at the fun memories we had of our childhoods.

My wonderful son, Adam, is my little rock. His love has helped me so much, especially his random cuddles on days when I didn't even realise how much I needed them.

Finally, I'd like to thank my mam, Rosaleen Dunne, for supporting me in writing this book and for her great support for me in general. She has had a lot of patience with me while I've been on this emotional rollercoaster. No matter how big or small my hurts have been, she has always come to my rescue. We talk about everything – sometimes I've told her too much. Some days we just sit in silence while she distracts me by playing one of my favourite board games: Scrabble. She's not just my mam; she's a best friend.

Orla

A number of people provided invaluable help with aspects of the research for this book:

I'd like to especially thank Gerry Curran and Bernard Regan of the Courts Service, and former chief registrar of the High Court, Kevin O'Neill.

Mary Carolan's thorough, authoritative journalism from the courts for the *Irish Times*, over several decades, has left an important historical archive of contemporaneous court reporting.

Without Gwen Malone Stenography there would not be a full record of the judgment in the Miss D case. We are very grateful that her company's work made sure such a record existed and that she was able to help me find it.

Míle buíochas leis an stiúrthóir, Paddy Hayes, agus an

léiritheoir, Aisling Ní Fhlaithearta, a dhéanann sárobair le paisean agus ionracas.

I'm extremely grateful to Sarah Liddy and Aoibheann Molumby and everyone at Gill Books for their editorial expertise, their compassion and their innate understanding of the importance of Amy's story from the start.

This book would not have been finished without the kindness of Aoibheann Téjan and her 'writing place'.

I'd like to thank my colleagues and friends for their support, encouragement and assistance, especially Vivienne Traynor, Aoife Kavanagh, Annette O'Donnell, Paul Reynolds, Sinead Crowley, Dearbhail McDonald, Nicola Donnelly, Frank Greaney, Susan Keogh, Ann O'Loughlin, Nina Noonan, Fiona O'Sullivan, Niamh Ryan, Simone Cosgrave, Laura Holmer and Jenny Huggard.

I am very grateful to James McNamara and the wonderful Kate and Cian for their patience with 'the book'.

Finally, thank you to Amy Dunne and her mother, Rosaleen, for their courage, resilience, warmth and honesty.